SHAKESPEARE'S

HISTORY OF

PERICLES, PRINCE OF TYRE

SHAKESPEARE'S

HISTORY OF

PERICLES, PRINCE OF TYRE.

WILLIAM SHAKESPEARE

EDITED, WITH NOTES,

BY

WILLIAM J. ROLFE, LITT. D.

GYAN

Published by

GYAN

Gyan Publishing House
5, Ansari Road
Daryaganj, New Delhi-110002
Phone: 011-47034999, 9811692060
E-mail: books@gyanbooks.com

Distribution Network
gyanbooks.com
India, USA, Canada, UK, Australia

ISBN: 978-81-212-8400-4 (HB)
First Published, 1609

2nd Impression 2024

Printed at: Gyan Press, Delhi.

SHAKESPEARE'S HISTORY OF PERICLES, PRINCE OF TYRE
Author: WILLIAM SHAKESPEARE EDITOR: WILLIAM J. ROLFE

PERICLES.

SHAKESPEARE'S

HISTORY OF

PERICLES, PRINCE OF TYRE.

EDITED, WITH NOTES,

BY

WILLIAM J. ROLFE, LITT. D.,

FORMERLY HEAD MASTER OF THE HIGH SCHOOL, CAMBRIDGE, MASS.

WITH ENGRAVINGS.

NEW YORK ·:· CINCINNATI ·:· CHICAGO

AMERICAN BOOK COMPANY

ENGLISH CLASSICS.

EDITED BY WM. J. ROLFE, LITT.D.

Illustrated. 12mo, Cloth, 56 cents per volume.

SHAKESPEARE'S WORKS.

The Merchant of Venice.
Othello.
Julius Cæsar.
A Midsummer-Night's Dream.
Macbeth.
Hamlet.
Much Ado about Nothing.
Romeo and Juliet.
As You Like It.
The Tempest.
Twelfth Night.
The Winter's Tale.
King John.
Richard II.
Henry IV. Part I.
Henry IV. Part II.
Henry V.
Henry VI. Part I.
Henry VI. Part II.
Henry VI. Part III.
Richard III.
Henry VIII.
King Lear.
The Taming of the Shrew.
All 's Well that Ends Well.
Coriolanus.
The Comedy of Errors.
Cymbeline.
Antony and Cleopatra.
Measure for Measure.
Merry Wives of Windsor.
Love's Labour 's Lost.
Two Gentlemen of Verona.
Timon of Athens.
Troilus and Cressida.
Pericles, Prince of Tyre.
The Two Noble Kinsmen.
Venus and Adonis, Lucrece, etc.
Sonnets.
Titus Andronicus.

GOLDSMITH'S SELECT POEMS.
GRAY'S SELECT POEMS.
MINOR POEMS OF JOHN MILTON.
BROWNING'S SELECT POEMS.
BROWNING'S SELECT DRAMAS.
MACAULAY'S LAYS OF ANCIENT ROME.
WORDSWORTH'S SELECT POEMS.

LAMBS' TALES FROM SHAKESPEARE'S COMEDIES.
LAMBS' TALES FROM SHAKESPEARE'S TRAGEDIES.
EDITED BY WM. J. ROLFE, LITT.D.
Illustrated. Cloth, 12mo, 50 cents per volume.

Pericles.
W. P. 6

PREFACE.

It was at first my intention to print in this edition only Shakespeare's part of *Pericles*; but, on second thought, I concluded to give the other portions in smaller type, as in *Timon of Athens*. The wretched brothel scenes in act iv. have been freely abridged, not because I suppose that the play will be read in schools, but because the scenes are not worth printing at all, except for the critical student, who of course has other and "unexpurgated" editions. My aim was to pick out from the nastiness no more than might serve to show the plan of the scenes and their relation to the rest of the play.

The illustrations are mostly from Knight's "Pictorial Shakspere."

CONTENTS.

THE PALACE AT ANTIOCH (I. I).

INTRODUCTION

TO

PERICLES, PRINCE OF TYRE.

I. THE HISTORY OF THE PLAY.

Pericles, Prince of Tyre, was first published in quarto in 1609, with the following title-page (as given in the Cambridge edition):

THE LATE, | And much admired Play, | Called | Pericles, Prince | of Tyre. | With the true Relation of the whole Historie, | aduentures, and fortunes of the said Prince: | As also, | The no lesse strange, and worthy accidents, | in the Birth and Life, of his Daughter | *MARIANA.* | As it hath been diuers and sundry times acted by | his Maiesties Seruants, at the Globe on | the Banck-side. | By William Shakespeare. | Imprinted at London for *Henry Gosson*, and are |

to be sold at the signe of the Sunne in | Pater-noster row, &c. | 1609.

Another edition, with the same title-page, was issued in the same year. It has generally been supposed that there was but one edition, and that the discrepancies between the copies were due to printers' corrections made while the sheets were passing through the press; but the Cambridge editors are satisfied from a careful examination of the different copies that there were really two distinct editions, and that it is possible to determine which was the earlier.*

A third quarto edition (of which there is a unique copy in the British Museum) appeared in 1611. The title-page is the same as that of the quartos of 1609, except for one or two slight variations in spelling and the imprint, which reads, "Printed at London by *S. S.* | 1611." It is apparently printed from a copy of the 2d quarto.

A fourth quarto bears the imprint, "Printed for *T. P.* 1619." The "signatures" of this edition are a continuation of those of *The Whole Contention between the two Famous Houses, Lancaster and Yorke,* printed without date but for the same publisher, Thomas Pavier (see our ed. of 2 *Henry VI.*, p. 10), showing that the two plays originally formed parts of the same volume.

A fifth quarto was brought out in 1630, some copies of which have the imprint: "LONDON, | Printed by *I. N.* for *R. B.* and are to be sould | at his shop in *Cheapside,* at the signe of the | *Bible.* 1630."; while others have simply "*LONDON,* | Printed by *J. N.* for *R. B.* 1630." In all other respects the latter are identical with the former.

A sixth quarto (printed from the fourth) has the imprint, "Printed at *London* by *Thomas Cotes,* 1635."

* Copies of the 1st edition, according to the Cambridge editors, are found in the Bodleian Library, in the Capell Collection, and in the British Museum; of the 2d edition, in the Duke of Devonshire's library, in the British Museum, and in the Public Library at Hamburg.

Pericles was not included in either the 1st or the 2d folio, but was reprinted, with several plays wrongly attributed to Shakespeare, in the 3d folio (1664), and in the 4th (1685). The folio text is taken from that of the 6th quarto.

Rowe included *Pericles* in both his editions (1709 and 1714), but it was rejected by Pope and subsequent editors down to the time of Malone, who put it in his Supplement to Steevens's edition of 1778, and in his edition of 1790. Steevens followed his example in 1793, and has been followed by all the recent editors with the exception of Keightley.*

It is now, however, generally agreed by the critics that the first two acts of the play, together with the brothel scenes in the fourth act, were written by some other author than Shakespeare. "What remains is the pure and charming romance of Marina, the sea-born child of Pericles, her loss, and the recovery of both child and mother by the afflicted prince" (Dowden). Whether the poet enlarged and reconstructed an earlier play, or some other writer or writers filled out an unfinished work of his, we cannot positively decide, but the latter seems by far the more reasonable hypothesis. This view has been ably set forth by Fleay in a paper the greater part of which is reprinted below.

The date of the play in its present form is probably about 1607. It was first printed, as we have seen, in 1609, but it was entered on the Stationers' Registers on the 20th of May, 1608. If, as Fleay tells us (*Introd. to Shakes. Study*, p. 28), the second scene of the third act is "palpably imitated in *The Puritan* (iv. 3)," which was acted in 1606, the date of *Pericles* cannot be later than that year.

II. THE SOURCES OF THE PLOT.

The story upon which the play is founded is given in Lau-

* For a fuller account of modern critical opinion concerning the play, see the extract from Verplanck below.

rence Twine's *Patterne of Painefull Aduenters*, first published in 1576, and in the tale of *Appolinus the Prince of Tyr*, which forms a part of Gower's *Confessio Amantis*. Twine's novel is said to have been merely a reprint of the English translation (printed in 1510) of the French version of the story by Robert Copland. It was taken originally from the *Gesta Romanorum*, but the narrative there was only one of three Latin versions, all of which appear to have been based on a Greek tale of the fifth or sixth century of the Christian era. Gower acknowledges his indebtedness to

"a cronique in daies gone,
The wich is cleped Panteon;"

that is, the Latin *Pantheon* of Godfrey of Viterbo, who wrote in the latter half of the 12th century.

In 1608 George Wilkins published a novel which was avowedly based on the acted play. The title-page was as follows:

THE | Painfull Aduentures | of *Pericles* Prince of | Tyre. | Being | The true History of the Play of *Pericles*, as it was | lately presented by the worthy and an- | cient Poet *Iohn Gower.* | AT LONDON | *Printed by T. P. for* Nat: Butter, | 1608.

We may fairly infer from the language of this title-page that the play was then a comparatively new one, and that the date given above (1607, or possibly 1606) cannot be far astray.

III. CRITICAL COMMENTS ON THE PLAY.

[*From Verplanck's "Shakespeare."* *]

The literary history of this play, and of the varying critical opinions respecting it, is curious. *Pericles* was a very popular play during the whole of Shakespeare's dramatic career; it was often acted at the "Globe," by the company in which

* *The Illustrated Shakespeare*, edited by G. C. Verplanck (New York, 1847), vol. iii. p. 5 of *Pericles*.

he had an interest, where (from the frequency of contemporary allusions to it) it seems to have been what is now called a *stock play.* Two successive editions of it, in the small quarto pamphlet form, then in use for such publications, were published during his life, and two or more within a few years after his death (1619 and 1630), all bearing his name as the author. It was, however, not contained in the first folio collection of his dramatic works, in 1623. It was afterwards inserted in the collection known as the "third folio," in 1664. During the whole of that century, there appears abundant contemporary evidence that *Pericles* was indeed, as its title-pages assert it to have been, a "much-admired play." Ben Jonson growled at it as "a mouldy tale," made up of "scraps out of every dish." But this was when, prematurely old, poor, and mortified at public injustice, he poured forth his "just indignation at the vulgar censure of his play, by malicious spectators;" and in doing so he bears strong testimony that the public judgment as to *Pericles* was the reverse of his own—that it "kept up the play-club," and was the favourite dramatic repast to the exclusion of his own "well-ordered banquet," in what he denounced as "a loathsome age," when

> "sweepings do as well
> As the best-ordered meal;
> For who the relish of such guests would fit,
> Needs set them but the alms-basket of wit."
>
> (Ben Jonson's *Ode to Himself*—"Come, leave the loathed stage," etc.)

Ben's frank and friendly admonitor, the moralist Owen Feltham, replies by reminding him that there were scenes and jokes in his own unfortunate play (the *New Inn*), that

> "throw a stain
> Through all the unlikely plot, and do displease
> As deep as *Pericles;*"

thus giving an additional testimony that the faults of *Pericles* did not escape the critical eye, while they pleased the many. Thus it kept possession of the stage to the days of Addison, when *Pericles* was one of the favourite parts of Betterton. Dryden, who lived near enough the author's time to have learned the stage tradition from contemporaries, while he evidently perceived the imperfections of this piece, never doubted its authenticity, and accounted for its inferiority to the greater tragedies, by considering them the consequences of the author's youthful inexperience:

> "Shakespeare's own muse her *Pericles* first bore;
> The Prince of Tyre was elder than the Moor:
> 'T is miracle to see a first good play;
> All hawthorns do not bloom on Christmas day."
>
> (Prologue to Davenant's *Circe*, 1675.)

This was in 1675, and the reputation of *Pericles*, and its unquestioned filiation as by Shakespeare, remained undisturbed until Rowe's edition, in 1709. Rowe had, upon some theory of his own, adopted the wild idea that Shakespeare, by the pure force of genius, attained at once to his highest excellence, without passing through the ordinary apprenticeship even of self-formed authors, in acquiring the command of words, style, versification, and invention, as well as taste, skill, and judgment, by persevering trial and experience. He thought, on the contrary, that "perhaps we are not to look for his beginnings, like those of other authors, among their least perfect writings: art had so little and nature so large a share in what he did, that, for aught I know, the performances of his youth, as they were the most vigorous, and had the most fire and strength of imagination in them, were the best." In consonance with this notice, he seems to have rejected the traditional opinion that *Pericles* was "a performance of the poet's youth," and instead of it makes the assertion that "it is owned that some part of *Pericles* was written by him, particularly the last scene;" thus intimating that the rest was from an inferior hand. He accordingly omitted the play in his editions, in which he was followed by the next succeeding editors. Pope's edition was the next in order, and the poet-critic, in his preface, made "no doubt that these *wretched plays, Pericles, Locrine, Sir John Oldcastle*, etc., etc., cannot be admitted as his." On the authority of these two poets, and especially of Pope, whom his admiring friend and successor in the editorial chair, Warburton, praised for his skill in selecting Shakespeare's genuine passages and works from the spurious ones, *Pericles* was summarily ejected from all the succeeding editions, those of Warburton, Theobald, Hanmer, and Johnson, as well as the common popular editions, without comment; so that, during the greater part of the last century, it was entirely unknown to the ordinary admirers of Shakespeare. Even Theobald, the bitter enemy and often the sagacious corrector of Pope, did not venture to dissent from the general decision, though he perceived and acknowledged in the play the traces of the master's hand. During this period, *Pericles* was noticed by critics and writers upon the English drama, only as a play once erroneously attributed to Shakespeare, and was as little known among literary men as any of the plays of the secondary dramatists of the same age, who have since been made familiar, at least by name and in quotation, by the brilliant comments of Lamb and Hazlitt, and the large use made of them by the commentators.

Towards the end of the century, *Pericles* appeared in the editions of Malone, and in those of Johnson and Steevens, after the associations of these two critics. This was mainly in consequence of the opinion maintained by Malone, who had the courage to assert and support by argument, that "*Pericles* was the entire work of Shakespeare, and one of his earliest compositions." Steevens, on the other hand, resolutely maintained:

"The drama before us contains no discrimination of manners (except in the comic dialogues), very few traces of original thought, and is evidently destitute of that intelligence and useful knowledge that pervade even the meanest of

Shakespeare's undisputed performances. To speak more plainly, it is neither enriched by the gems that sparkle through the rubbish of *Love's Labour 's Lost*, nor the good sense which so often fertilizes the barren fable of the *Two Gentlemen of Verona*. *Pericles*, in short, is little more than a string of adventures so numerous, so inartificially crowded together, and so far removed from probability, that, in my private judgment, I must acquit even the irregular and lawless Shakespeare of having constructed the fabric of the drama, though he has certainly bestowed some decoration on its parts. Yet even this decoration, like embroidery on a blanket, only serves by contrast to expose the meanness of the original materials. That the plays of Shakespeare have their inequalities likewise, is sufficiently understood; but they are still the inequalities of Shakespeare. He may occasionally be absurd, but is seldom foolish; he may be censured, but can rarely be despised.

"I do not recollect a single plot of Shakespeare's formation (or even adoption from preceding plays or novels), in which the majority of the characters are not so well connected, and so necessary in respect of each other, that they proceed in combination to the end of the story; unless the story (as in the cases of Antigonus and Mercutio) requires the interposition of death. In *Pericles* this continuity is wanting:

> 'disjectas moles, avulsaque saxis
> Saxa vides;"

and even with the aid of Gower the scenes are rather loosely tacked together than closely interwoven. We see no more of Antiochus after his first appearance. His anonymous daughter utters but one unintelligible couplet, and then vanishes. Simonides likewise is lost as soon as the marriage of Thaisa is over; and the punishment of Cleon and his wife, which poetic justice demanded, makes no part of the action, but is related in a kind of epilogue by Gower. This is at least a practice which in no instance has received the sanction of Shakespeare. From such deficiency of mutual interest and *liaison* among the personages of the drama, I am further strengthened in my belief that our great poet had no share in constructing it. Dr. Johnson long ago observed that his *real* power is not seen in the splendour of particular passages, but in the progress of his fable, and the tenour of his dialogue; and when it becomes necessary for me to quote a decision founded on comprehensive views, I can appeal to none in which I should more implicitly confide. Gower relates the story of Pericles in a manner not quite so desultory; and yet such a tale as that of Prince Appolyn, in its most perfect state, would hardly have attracted the notice of any playwright, except one who was quite a novice in the rules of his art."

In this view Malone finally acquiesced, in substance, though, with great truth and good taste, still insisting that "the wildness and irregularity of the fable, the artless conduct of the piece, and the inequalities of the poetry, may be all accounted for, by supposing it either his first or one of his earliest essays in dramatic composition."

Steevens's decision long remained unquestioned, both as to the point of Shakespeare's share of authorship, and the poetic merits of the drama itself; and it has recently received more authority for having been substantially reaffirmed by Mr. Hallam: "From the poverty and bad management of the fable, the want of effective and distinguishable character, and the general feebleness of the tragedy as a whole, I should not believe the structure to have been Shakespeare's. But (he adds) many passages are far more in his manner than in that of any contemporary writer with whom I am acquainted, and the extrinsic testimony, though not conclusive, being of some value, I should not dissent from the judgment of Steevens and Malone, that it was in 'no inconsiderable degree repaired and improved by his hand'"

(*Literature of Europe*). He elsewhere insists that "the play is full of evident marks of an inferior hand." Other modern critics, of nearly as high name, have gone still further in censure: W. Gifford, for example, rejects and brands the play as "the worthless *Pericles.*"

This sweeping, unqualified censure was amusingly counterbalanced by as unqualified an expression of admiration, by William Godwin—a writer whose political ethics and metaphysics, full of the boldest opinions, expressed in the most startling and paradoxical form, had prepared the public to expect similar extravagances on all other subjects, and had thus taken away much of the weight of his literary judgments. Yet these judgments are in fact entitled to all the weight due to a writer of genius,—manifesting on all such subjects an extensive acquaintance with English literature in its whole range, guided by a pure taste, and a quick and deep sensibility to every form of beauty. In his *Life of Chaucer*, incidentally speaking of *Pericles*, he designates it as "a beautiful drama, which in sweetness of manner, delicacy of description, truth of feeling, and natural ease of language, would do honour to the greatest author that ever existed." Since that period, many others have been more disposed to dwell upon the beauties of *Pericles*—the existence of which few now deny—than upon its many defects, to which none but a blind idolater of the great bard can close his eyes. Accordingly its merits have been vindicated by the modern continental critics, and by several of the later English ones: as by Franz Horn, Ulrici, Knight, Dr. Drake, and especially by Mr. Procter (Barry Cornwall), in a long and admirable note, in his memoir of Ben Jonson, prefixed to Moxon's edition of Jonson's works (1838). Barry Cornwall roundly charges the preceding critics (from Pope to Gifford) with having condemned *Pericles unread;* while he proves that "the merit and style of the work sufficiently denote the author"—that author of whom he eloquently says, that he "was and is, beyond all competition, the greatest poet that the world has ever seen. He is the greatest in general power, and greatest in style, which is symbol or evidence of power. For the motion of verse corresponds with the power of the poet; as the swell and tumult of the sea answer to the winds that call them up. From *Lear* down to *Pericles*, there ought to be no mistake between Shakespeare and any other writer."

The "glorious uncertainty of the law" has been exemplified and commemorated, in a large and closely printed volume, containing nothing but the mere titles of legal decisions, once acknowledged as law, and since reversed or contradicted, as "cases overruled, doubted, or denied." The decisions of the critical tribunals would furnish materials for a much larger work; and Shakespearian criticism, by itself, would supply an ample record of varying or overruled judgments. Those on the subject of *Pericles* alone would constitute a large title in the collection.

Yet, in the play itself may be found some foundation for all and each of those opinions, though least for the hasty and vague censures of Pope and Gifford. The play is awkwardly and unskilfully constructed, being on the plan of the old legendary drama, when it was thought sufficient to put some popular narrative into action, with little attempt at a condensed and sustained continuous interest in the plot or its personages. It rambles along through the period of two generations, without any attempt at the artist-like management of a similar duration in the *Winter's Tale*, by breaking up the story into parts, and making the one a natural sequel to the other, so as to keep up a uniform continuity of interest throughout both. The story itself is extravagant, and its denouement is caused by the aid of the heathen mythology, which every mind, trained under modern associations and habits of thought, feels as repugnant to dramatic truth, and at once refuses to lend to it that transient conventional belief so necessary to any degree of illusion or interest, and so readily given to shadowy superstitions of other kinds, as ghosts, witches, and fairies, more akin to our general opinions, or more familiar to our childhood. A still greater defect than this is one rare indeed in any thing from Shakespeare's mind—the vagueness and meagreness of the characters, undistinguished by any of that portrait-like individuality which gives life and reality to the humblest personages of his scene. Thence, in spite of the excellence of particular parts, there results a general feebleness of effect in the whole. The versification is, in general, singularly halting and uncouth, and the style is sometimes creeping and sometimes extravagant.

From these circumstances, if, at the time when *Pericles* was excluded from the ordinary editions, its place had been supplied by a prose outline of the story, with occasional specimens of the dialogue, such as Voltaire gave of *Julius Cæsar*, selected only from the most extravagant passages, there would be little hesitation in denying the whole or the greater part of the play to be Shakespeare's, or in allowing that it bore "evident marks of an inferior hand."

Yet, on the other hand, it contains much to please, to surprise, to affect, and to delight. The introduction of old Gower, linking together the broken action by his antiquated legendary narrative, is original and pleasing. The very first scenes have here and there some passages of sudden and unexpected grandeur, and the later acts bear everywhere the very "form and pressure" of Shakespeare's mind. Yet it is observable, that wherever we meet him, in his own unquestionable person, it is not as the poetic Shakespeare of the youthful comedies, but with the port and style of the author of *Lear* and *Cordelia*. Indeed, the scene, in the last act, of Pericles's recognition of his daughter, recalls strongly the touching passages of Cordelia's filial love, and Lear's return to reason, by a resemblance, not so much of situation or language, as of spirit and feeling. The language and style of these nobler passages are peculiarly Shakespearian, and, as Mr. Hallam justly observes, "of the poet's later manner." They have his emphatic mode of employing the plainest and most homely words in the highest and most poetical sense,—his original compounds, his crowded magnificence of gorgeous imagery, interspersed with the simplest touches of living nature. Thus, when Pericles retraces his lost wife's features in his recovered child:

"My dearest wife was like this maid, and such a one
My daughter might have been; my queen's square brows,
Her stature to an inch; as wand-like straight;
As silver-voïc'd; her eyes as jewel-like,
And cas'd as richly; in pace another Juno;
Who starves the ears she feeds, and makes them hungry
The more she gives them speech."

Here, too, we find his peculiar mode of stating and enforcing general truths—not in didactic digression, but as interwoven with and growing out of the incidents or passing emotions of the scene. Taking these characteristics into view, and these alone, the play must be pronounced worthy of all the praise bestowed by Godwin. If, then, we were to reverse the experiment, just suggested, upon the supposed reader who knows no more of *Pericles* than that it is a play which has been ascribed by some to Shakespeare, and to place before him a prose abstract of the plot, interspersed with large extracts from the finer passages, he would surely wonder why there could have been a moment's hesitation in placing *Pericles* by the side of *Cymbeline* and the *Winter's Tale.*

There are two different solutions of these contradictory phenomena, and it is not easy to decide, with confidence, which is the true one. The first hypothesis is founded upon the old traditionary opinion, that *Pericles*, in its original form, was one of the author's earliest dramatic essays, perhaps an almost boyish work; but that not long before 1609, when it was printed as a "late much-admired play," the author, then in the meridian of his reputation, revised and enlarged it, as he had repeatedly done with others of his plays, which, like *Romeo and Juliet*, *Love's Labour's Lost*, etc., are announced in their title-pages as having been "newly corrected, augmented, and amended." This hypothesis, of course, rejects the favourite notion that Shakespeare's genius burst forth at once in its full splendour and magnitude, and takes for granted, what all experience teaches, that the first trials of his strength had the awkwardness and feebleness of boyish youth. This hypothesis corresponds with the legendary and inartificial structure of the main story, and the feebleness of characterization—points which would be least of all susceptible of improvement, without an entire recasting of the drama. It agrees, too, with the large stage-direction and ample allowance of dumb show, such as he afterwards introduced into his mimic play in *Hamlet*, and as remain in *Cymbeline* as remnants of the old groundwork of that drama, and which were strongly characteristic of the fashion of the stage in Shakespeare's youth. The additions and improvements are very perceptible, and stand out boldly from the weakly executed framework of the drama, which remains untouched—differing from similar enlargements and corrections of others of his own dramas (as *Romeo and Juliet*, etc.) by the poet himself, in the greater contrast here afforded by the effusions of his matured mind with the timid outline of his unpractised hand; and differing again from *Cymbeline* (as Coleridge remarks) by the "entire *rifacimento* of the latter, when Shakespeare's celebrity as a poet, no less than his influence as manager, enabled him to bring forward the lordly labours of his youth." *Pericles* having, from its first appearance, by means of its story, its dumb-show, and by its comparative merit relatively to its rivals for popular favour, succeeded and kept possession of the stage, the author would not feel himself called upon to rewrite a play which answered its main end, and the subject of which presented no peculiar attractions to him, while the re-examination of his own boyish, half-formed thoughts would naturally expand and elevate them into nobler forms, and reclothe them in that glowing language he had since created for himself.

This theory commends itself as every way probable to my judgment, as it has done to that of others, whose opinions are entitled to great deference.

Nevertheless, the other solution of the difficulty—that proposed by Mr. Hallam—may still be the true one: that the original *Pericles* was by some inferior hand, perhaps by a personal friend of Shakespeare's, and that he, without remodelling the plot, undertook to correct and improve it, beginning with slight additions, and his mind, warming as he proceeded, breaking out towards the close of the drama with its accustomed vigour and abundance.

This opinion has been the more generally received one among the English critics, and it has the advantage of solving one difficulty which the other theory leaves unexplained —why *Pericles* was omitted by the editors of the first folio.

[*From Knight's "Pictorial Shakspere."* *]

We call the play before us by the name of *Pericles*, because it was so called in the first rudely printed copies, and because the contemporaries of the writer, following the printed copies, so called it in their printed books. But Malone has given us an epigram of Richard Flecknoe, 1670, "On the Play of the Life of *Pyrocles.*" There can be little doubt, we think, as Steevens has very justly argued, that Pyrocles was the name of the hero of this play. For who was Pyrocles? The hero of Sidney's *Arcadia.* Steevens says, "It is remarkable that many of our ancient writers were ambitious to exhibit Sidney's worthies on the stage; and when his subordinate

* *Doubtful Plays*, etc. (2d ed. 1867), p. 117 fol. (by permission).

agents were advanced to such honour, how happened it that Pyrocles, their leader, should be overlooked?" To a young poet, who probably had access to the *Arcadia* in manuscript before its publication in 1590, the name of Pyrocles would naturally present itself as worthy to succeed the somewhat unmanageable Appollinus of Gower; and that name would recommend itself to an audience who, if they were of the privileged circles, such as the actors of the Blackfriars often addressed, were familiar with the *Arcadia* before its publication. After 1590 the *Arcadia* was the most popular work of the age.

It will be seen, then, that we advocate the belief that *Pyrocles*, or *Pericles*, was a very early work of Shakspere, in some form, however, different from that which we possess. That it was an early work we are constrained to believe; not from the evidence of particular passages, which may be deficient in power or devoid of refinement, but from the entire construction of the dramatic action. The play is essentially one of movement, which is a great requisite for dramatic success; but that movement is not held in subjection to a unity of idea. The writer, in constructing the plot, had not arrived to a perfect conception of the principle "that a tragedy is tied to the laws of poesy, and not of history, not bound to follow the story, but having liberty either to feign a quite new matter, or to frame the history to the most tragical convenience." But with this essential disadvantage we cannot doubt that, even with very imperfect dialogue, the action presented a succession of scenes of very absorbing interest. The introduction of Gower, however inartificial it may seem, was the result of very profound skill. The presence of Gower supplied the unity of idea which the desultory nature of the story wanted; and thus it is that, in "the true history" formed upon the play, the unity of idea is kept in the expression of the title-page, "as it was lately presented by the worthy and ancient poet, John Gower."

Nevertheless, such a story we believe could not have been chosen by Shakspere in the seventeenth century, when his art was fully developed in all its wondrous powers and combinations. With his perfect mastery of the faculty of representing, instead of recording, the treatment of a story which would have required perpetual explanation and connection would have been painful to him, if not impossible.

Dr. Drake has bestowed very considerable attention upon the endeavour to prove that *Pericles* ought to be received as the indisputable work of Shakspere. Yet his arguments, after all, amount only to the establishment of the following theory: "No play, in fact, more openly discloses the hand of Shakspeare than *Pericles*, and fortunately his share in its composition appears to have been very considerable; he may be distinctly, though not frequently, traced in the first and second acts; after which, *feeling the incompetency of his fellow-labourer*, he seems to have assumed almost the entire management of the remainder, nearly the whole of the third, fourth, and fifth acts bearing indisputable testimony to the genius and execution of the great master."* This theory of companionship in the production of the play is merely a repetition of the theory of Steevens: "The *purpurei panni* are Shakspeare's, and the rest the productions of some inglorious and forgotten playwright." We have no faith whatever in this very easy mode of disposing of the authorship of a doubtful play—of leaving entirely out of view the most important part of every drama, its action, its characterization, looking at the whole merely as a collection of passages, of which the worst are to be assigned to some *âme damnée*, and the best triumphantly claimed for Shakspere. There are some, however, who judge of such matters upon broader principles. Mr. Hallam says, "*Pericles* is generally reckoned to be in part, and only in part, the work of Shakspeare. From the poverty and bad management of the fable, the

* *Shakspeare and his Times*, vol. ii. p. 268.

want of any effective or distinguishable character, for Marina is no more than the common form of female virtue, such as all the dramatists of that age could draw, and a general feebleness of the tragedy as a whole, I should not believe the structure to have been Shakspeare's. But many passages are far more in his manner than in that of any contemporary writer with whom I am acquainted."* Here "the poverty and bad management of the fable"—"the want of any effective or distinguishable character"—are assigned for the belief that the structure could not have been Shakspere's. But let us accept Dryden's opinion that

"Shakspeare's own muse his Pericles first bore,"

with reference to the original structure of the play, and the difficulty vanishes. It was impossible that the character of the early drama should not have been impressed upon Shakspere's earliest efforts. Sidney has given us a most distinct description of that drama; and we can thus understand how the author of *Pericles* improved upon what he found. Do we therefore think that the drama, as it has come down to us, is presented in the form in which it was first written? By no means. We agree with Mr. Hallam that in parts the language seems rather that of Shakspere's "second or third manner than of his first." But this belief is not inconsistent with the opinion that the original structure was Shakspere's. No other poet that existed at the beginning of the seventeenth century—perhaps no poet that came after that period, whether Massinger, or Fletcher, or Webster—could have written the greater part of the fifth act. Coarse as the comic scenes are, there are touches in them unlike any other writer but Shakspere. Horn, with the eye of a real critic, has pointed out the deep poetical profundity of one apparently slight passage in these unpleasant scenes:

"*Marina.* Are you a woman?
Bawd. What would you have me be, an I be not a woman?
Marina. An honest woman, or not a woman."

* *History of Literature*, vol. iii. p. 569.

Touches such as these are not put into the work of other men. Who but Shakspere could have written

> "The blind mole casts
> Copp'd hills towards heaven, to tell, the earth is throng'd
> By man's oppression; and the poor worm doth die for 't."

And yet this passage comes naturally enough in a speech of no very high excellence. The *purpurei panni* must be fitted to a body, as well for use as for adornment. We think that Shakspere would not have taken the trouble to produce these costly robes for the decoration of what another had essentially created. We are willing to believe that, even in the very height of his fame, he would have bestowed any amount of labour for the improvement of an early production of his own, if the taste of his audiences had from time to time demanded its continuance upon the stage. It is for this reason that we think that the *Pericles* of the beginning of the seventeenth century was the revival of a play written by Shakspere some twenty years earlier.

[*From Fleay's* "*Shakespeare Manual.*" *]

With regard to the authorship of this play, we may, I think, take it at once for granted, that the first two acts are not by Shakespeare. It has been so long admitted by all critics of note that this is the case, that it cannot be worth while to go over the evidence again in detail. In order, however, to extinguish any lingering doubt, I give the metrical evidence; which will, at the same time, show how much more easily and certainly this result would have been arrived at had this method of investigation been earlier adopted. The play consists of verse scenes, prose scenes, and the Gower chorus. Considering at present only the first of these three parts, we shall find so marked a difference between the first two, and last three, acts, as to render

* *Shakespeare Manual*, by F. G. Fleay, M.A. (London, 1876), p. 209 fol. See also *Transactions of New Shakspere Society* for 1874, p. 195 fol.

it astonishing that they could ever have been supposed to be the work of one author.

COMPARATIVE TABLE.

	Acts i., ii.	Acts iii., iv., v.
Total No. of lines	835	827
No. of rhyme lines . . .	195	14
No. of double endings . .	72	106
No. of Alexandrines . . .	5	13
No. of short lines	71	98
No. of rhymes not dialogue	8	16

The differences in the other items are striking, and of themselves conclusive; but the difference of the numbers of rhymes, the proportion being 14 in the one part to 1 in the other, is such as the most careless critic ought to have long since noticed. With regard to this main question, then, there can be no doubt: the three last acts alone can be Shakespeare's; the other part is by some one of a very different school. But we have minor questions of some interest to settle. The first of these is, Who wrote the scenes in the brothel, act iv. sc. 2, 5, 6? I say decidedly, not Shakespeare; for these reasons: These scenes are totally unlike Shakespeare's in feeling on such matters. He would not have indulged in the morbid anatomy of such loathsome characters; he would have covered the ulcerous sores with a film of humour, if it were a necessary part of his moral surgery to treat them at all; and, above all, he would not have married Marina to a man whose acquaintance she had first made in a public brothel, to which *his* motives of resort were not recommendatory, however involuntary *her* sojourn there may have been. A still stronger argument is the omission of any allusion in the after-scenes to these three. In one place, indeed, there seems to be a contradiction of them. The after-account of Marina, which is amply sufficient without the prose scenes for dramatic purposes, is given thus:

> "We haue a *maid* in Metiline . . .
> She *with her fellow maides* [is] now upon
> The leauie shelter that abutts against
> The Islands side."—Act v. sc. 1.

I cannot reconcile this with

> "Proclaim that I can sing, weave, sowe, and dance,
> And [I] will undertake all these to teach."—Act iv. sc. 6.

nor with

> "Pupils lacks she none of nobler race,
> Who pour their bounty on her: and her gain
> *She gives the cursed Bawd.*"—Act v., *Gower.*

But if these scenes are not Shakespeare's (and repeated examination only strengthens my conviction that they are not), the clumsy Gower chorus is not his either. And this brings us to the only hypothesis that explains all the difficulties of this play. The usual hypothesis has been that Shakespeare finished a play begun by some one else: that is, that he deliberately chose a story of incest, which, having no tragic horror in it, would have been rejected by Ford or Massinger, and grafted on to this a filthy story, which, being void of humour, would even have been rejected by Fletcher. This arises from the fallacy which I noted in a previous paper, caused by the inveterate habit of beginning criticism from the first pages of a book, instead of from the easiest and most central standpoint. The theory which I propose as certain is this:—Shakespeare wrote the story of Marina, in the last three acts, minus the prose scenes and the Gower. This gives a perfect artistic and organic whole, and, in my opinion, ought to be printed as such in every edition of Shakespeare: the whole play, as it stands, might be printed in collections for the curious, and there only. But this story was not enough for filling the necessary five acts from which Shakespeare never deviated; he therefore left it unfinished, and used the arrangement of much of the later part in the end of *Winter's Tale*, which should be carefully compared with this play. The unfinished play was put into the hands of another of the "poets" attached to the same theatre, and the greater part of the present play was the result; this poet having used the whole story as given in Gower and elsewhere.

It is somewhat confirmatory of this theory that the play was not admitted into the 1st folio; nor published before 1623, except in quarto, first by Gosson, then by Pavier, whose dealings in *scarcely anything but* surreptitious editions are so conspicuous. It is difficult to understand how such poetry as is contained in the Shakespeare part of this play could have been neglected, had there not been some reason for the editors of the folio to leave it out of their edition; either some tradition of Shakespeare's disgust at the way in which his work had been completed, or some strong feeling that its publication in their authorized edition would be no credit to its author. One thing is certain, that it was absolutely neglected by Shakespeare himself: no play of his, however carelessly printed, has its text in so wretched a condition; nor has the way in which modern editors have arranged its verse—which is for the most part printed as prose in the old editions—been much more creditable to them than the disarrangement of it was to the older editors.

In confirmation for the general conclusions arrived at above, I may add a few isolated considerations. In the list of the actors' names, Boult, Bawd, and Pander are omitted: now these, and these only, are the additional characters introduced in the brothel scenes in the fourth act. This looks very much as if these scenes had been an afterthought added when the rest of the play had been already arranged. Couple with this the fact that the Gower parts in acts iv., v., in which these scenes are alluded to, are in lines of five measures, and not of four, as those in the earlier acts are: observe, also, that these scenes, though far from reaching to Shakespeare's excellence, are certainly superior to anything in the first two acts, so far as mere literature is concerned, and it will be almost certain that *three* authors were concerned in this play. The first author wrote the first two acts, and arranged the whole so as to incorporate the Shakespeare part. The second wrote the five-measure Gower parts and the brothel-scènes in acts iv., v., in order to lengthen out the play to the legitimate five acts. Even as it stands the play is far shorter than any play of Shakespeare's;* and it was probably in order to make up for the want of poetic invention that the long dumb-show performances were introduced into the Gower parts. It is scarcely possible to test the prose in the same way as we can the verse in these scenes; but even the little verse we have of the second writer's will, I think, be enough to confirm my theory. Not that the prose in act iv. is like that in acts i., ii.; but that the differences are not, by any test I have yet devised, capable of tabulation. I give specimens of the verse, for comparison.

I.—Shakespeare. His first piece in the play:

"Thou God of this great vast, rebuke these surges,
Which wash both heauen and hell; and thou, that hast
Vpon the windes commaund, bind them in Brasse,
Hauing [re]call'd them from the deepe; O still
Thy deafning, dreadfull thunders; gently quench
Thy nimble sulphirous flashes."—Act iii. sc. 1.

II.—Author of brothel scenes:

"Neither of these are so bad as thou art,
Since they do better thee in their command;
Thou hold'st a place for which the painedst fiend
In hell would not in reputation change:
Thou art the damnèd doorkeeper to every
Cusherel that comes enquiring for his Tib:

* *T. of A.*, *M. N. D.*, *Temp.*, *T. G. of V.*, *Macbeth*, and *C. of E.* are all shorter than *Pericles;* but Mr. Fleay writes us that he meant to say "any unabridged play," and all the above (except *T. of A.*, which is not wholly Shakespeare's) he believes to have been shortened for the stage.—*Ed.*

To the cholerick fisting of every rogue
Thy ear is liable: thy food is such
As hath been belcht on by infectious lungs."—Act iv. sc. 6.

III.—Arranger of whole piece:

"Yet cease your ire, you angry Stars of heaven,
Wind, Rain, and Thunder: Remember earthly man
Is but a substance that must yield to you:
And I, (as fits my nature,) do obey you.
Alas, the Seas hath cast me on the Rocks,
Washt me from shore to shore, and left my breath
Nothing to think on but ensuing death:
Let it suffice the greatnesse of your powers
To have bereft a Prince of all his fortunes,
And having thrown him from your watry grave,
Here to have death in peace is all he 'll crave."—Act ii. sc. 1.

These three styles are about as different as any can be, but still further to distinguish the non-Shakespearian writers, let us compare their rhyming-verse.

I.—Writer of brothel scenes:

"And *Pericles*, in sorrow all-devourd,
With sighes shot through, and biggest teares o'reshowr'd,
Leaves *Tharsus* and again imbarks, he sweares
Never to wash his face nor cut his haires,
He puts on Sackcloth and to Sea he beares,
A tempest which his mortall Vessell teares.
And yet he rides it out. Now take we our way
To the Epitaph for Marina writ by Dionizia,
The fairest, sweetest, and best lies here,
Who withered in her spring of year:
She was of *Tyrus* the King's Daughter,
On whom foule death hath made this slaughter:
Marina was she call'd, and at her birth
Thetis, being proud, swallow'd some part of th' earth:
Therefore the earth, fearing to be o'reflow'd
Hath *Thetis* birth-childe on the heav'ns bestow'd,
Wherefore she does & swears she 'll never stint,
Make raging Battry vpon shores of flint."—*Gower*, act iv.

Before, however, comparing this with passages from acts i. and ii., consider the monstrous theory which all the best critics, except Sidney Walker, have hitherto held.* Delius, for instance, in his preface to his translation of *Pericles* (in Bodenstedt's edition), says that "the original composer of this drama, later on, withdrew in favour of his co-worker Shakespeare—so to say, allowing himself to be eclipsed." Imagine Shakespeare in his best period allowing this stuff to stand in a play over which he had the full control! It is impossible. Shakespeare certainly never had any management or arrangement of the play: he only contributed the Marina story, which I have tried to separate and restore to him. Read that by itself: then turn to any of the other portions, and see how you like the flavour! But to return to our comparison. Take from act ii., Gower, this bit; note its affected and obsolete form, and see whether it is by the same hand as the last-quoted bit, which is almost modern in form and arrangement:

"By many a dearne and painfull pearch
Of Pericles, the carefull search,
By the four opposing Coignes,
Which the world together joynes,
Is made with all due diligence,
That horse and saile, and high expence,
Can steed the quest. At last from *Tyre*,
Fame answering the most strange enquire,
To th' Court of *King* Simonides
Are Letters brought, the tenour these."

And with the Epitaph compare *The Riddle* (act i. sc. 1):

"I am no Viper, yet I feed
On mother's flesh which did me breed:
I sought a husband, in which labour
I found that kindnesse in a father.
Hee 's father, sonne, and husbande mild,
I Mother, Wife, and yet his child.

* Walker held the theory of three authors, and rightly divided the play; but was certainly wrong in fixing on Dekker as the third man I did not know this when I wrote the text.

> How they may be, and yet in two,
> As you will live, resolve it you."

Surely we may conclude that there were three authors. But who were they?

The original manager and supervisor of the whole work was, as Delius says, George Wilkins; he made the play as far as he *wrote* it, from Twine's novel: he calls it "a poore infant of my braine;" he plumes himself on the arrangement of the Gower choruses as his own invention. In this, Delius is undoubtedly right; and to his preface I refer for further information on the matter. In confirmation, however, of this theory, I give an analysis of the metre of the only play of G. Wilkins which we possess—*The Miseries of Inforced Marriage*—which will be found to coincide very closely with that of acts i., ii. of *Pericles* given above, and which is more like it than that of any other play among the hundreds I have tabulated. There are in that play 526 rhyming lines, 155 double endings, 15 Alexandrines, 102 short lines, 14 rhyming lines of less than five measures, and a good deal of prose, which, seeing that the play is about three times the length of the first two acts of *Pericles*, gives a marvellously close agreement in percentage.

The second author was, I think, unquestionably W. Rowley. I have not just now access to complete plays of his in verse, but comparison of the prose with that of *A Match at Midnight*, and of the verse with that of the plays he wrote in conjunction with Fletcher and Massinger, assures me absolutely of the truth of this conjecture. Indeed, if I had complete plays of his in verse here, the quantity of verse in the *Pericles* by Rowley is too small to build a tabulation on. One peculiarity of his work, however, gives us a strong confirmation; it is always detached, and splits off from his coadjutors' with a clean cleavage.

In Fletcher's *Maid of the Mill*, the work of the two men might be published as two separate plays: so it is here.

Rowley's scenes are useful for no dramatic purpose, and might be cut out as cleanly as his characters have been from the list of the actors' names.

Since writing the above, I find that, just about the time that *Pericles* was written, GEORGE WILKINS was joined with John Day and W. ROWLEY in writing "*The Travels of the Three English brothers, Sir Thomas, Sir Anthony, and Sir Robert Shirley, an Historicall Play, printed in Quarto*, 1607." This makes assurance doubly sure, that ROWLEY and WILKINS were also joint writers in the *Pericles*. Moreover, the impudent use of Shakespeare's name in 1653 on the title-page of *The Birth of Merlin*, in conjunction with Rowley's, indicates a tradition that Shakespeare and Rowley had worked on the same piece or pieces at some period.

[*From Mr. F. J. Furnivall's Introduction to the Play.**]

This play forms a fit opening for the Fourth Period, in its happy reuniting of the long-separated family, father, mother, and daughter (Shakspere has now only two daughters, his son died in 1596), and in Pericles's flood of joy and gratitude at his finding wife and girl again, sweeping away all thought of his intended revenge on his wrongers, Dionyza and Cleon. *Pericles* is, like *Timon*, only partly from Shakspere's hand. He wrote only the last three acts, less the prose brothel scenes and the Gower choruses in them. As you read through the dull beginning acts, you at once feel the change of hand when you come on the first words of act iii.: "Thou god of this great vast." You see the birth of Marina, the supposed death and casting into the sea of her mother Thaisa, the committal of the babe to Cleon's treach erous wife Dionyza, the betrayal of her trust by that harpy, and her persuading Leonine to murder Marina simply because she was more beautiful than her own daughter. Then we see Marina rescued, but see, too, the despair of Pericles

* *The Leopold Shakspere* (London, 1877), p. lxxxvii. fol. (by permission).

on hearing of her (supposed) death, his three months' silence, and then his recovery under his daughter's earnest pleas:

> "Who starves the ears she feeds, and makes them hungry,
> The more she gives them speech."

And then his great "sea of joys" rushing upon him when he is convinced of her existence; then, his first thoughts of vengeance postponed, his visit to the Temple of Diana at Ephesus, the high-priestess, his wife Thaisa, recognising him, and thus finding husband and daughter at once: "*Per.* Ye gods, your present kindness makes my past misery," etc. Thenceforth he thinks only of their daughter's marriage; vengeance is forgotten in his joy. Shakspere's motive in taking up the story was surely this reunion of father, mother, and daughter, and not the early part, of Apollonius of Tyre's incest with his child, which Chaucer reproached Gower for telling. Still, he may have meant to show us Marina by her purity and virgin presence disarming the lust of men, thus giving us in her a Fourth-Period representative of the glorious Third-Period Isabella. Gower's version of the ancient legend was re-told in two prose forms in Shakspere's day, and an expression or two in the 1608 one, "poor inch of nature," etc., looks like Shakspere, and as if borrowed from a different version of the play to that which we now have. One passage in *Pericles* has for me a personal interest as regards Shakspere. Seeing with what contempt he treated the apothecaries in the *Errors* and *Romeo and Juliet*, and how little notice he took of the Doctor in *Macbeth*, we are struck with the very different character he gives to the noble, scientific, and generous Cerimon here. He is a man working for the good of all, the kind of man that Bacon would have desired for a friend. And recollecting that the date of this play is 1608 (or 1607), I cannot help believing that Cerimon represents to some extent the famous Stratford physician, Dr. John Hall, who, on June 5, 1607, married Shakspere's eldest daughter Susanna.

NOTE BY THE EDITOR.—In the discussion which followed the reading of Mr. Fleay's paper on *Pericles* before the New Shakspere Society, May 8, 1874, Mr. Furnivall remarked (see *Trans. of N. S. Soc.* for 1874, p. 252):

"I hope the fact I am going to mention will render all further discussion as to the Shakspere part of the *Pericles* unnecessary. When I first saw Mr. Tennyson last winter—after many years' occasional correspondence—he asked me, during our talk, whether I had ever examined *Pericles* with any care. I had to confess that I 'd never read it, as some friends whom I considered good judges had told me it was very doubtful whether Shakspere wrote any of it. Mr. Tennyson answered, 'Oh, that won't do. He wrote all the part relating to the birth and recovery of Marina, and the recovery of Thais. I settled that long ago. Come up-stairs, and I 'll read it to you.' Up-stairs to the smoking-room in Seamore Place we went, and there I had the rare treat of hearing the poet read in his deep voice—with an occasional triumphant 'Is n't *that* Shakspere? what do you think of that?' and a few comments—the genuine part of *Pericles*. I need not tell you how I enjoyed the reading, or how quick and sincere my conviction of the genuineness of the part read was."

The parts read by Tennyson were almost exactly the same that Mr. Fleay had marked as Shakespeare's; and, as Mr. Furnivall adds, "the independent confirmation of the poet-critic's result by the metrical-test worker's process is most satisfactory and interesting."

[*From Dowden's "Shakspere Primer."* *]

The drama as a whole is singularly undramatic. It entirely lacks unity of action, and the prominent figures of the opening scenes quickly drop out of the play. A main part of the story is briefly told in rhymed verse by the presenter, Gower, or is set forth in dumb show. But Shakspere's part is one and indivisible. It opens on shipboard with a tempest, and in Shakspere's later play of storm and wreck he has not attempted to rival the earlier treatment of the subject. "No poetry of shipwreck and the sea," a living poet writes, "has ever equalled the great scene of *Pericles;* no such note of music was ever struck out of the clash and contention of tempestuous elements." Milton, when writing

* *Literature Primers: Shakspere*, by Edward Dowden, LL.D. (London, 1878), p. 145 fol.

Lycidas, the elegy upon his drowned friend, remembered this scene, and one line in particular: "When humming water shall o'erwhelm thy corpse." To this rage of storm succeeds the hush of Cerimon's studious chamber, in which the wife of Pericles, tossed ashore by the waves, wakens wonderingly from her trance to the sound of melancholy music. Cerimon, who is master of the secrets of nature, who is liberal in his "learned charity," who held it ever

> "Virtue and cunning were endowments greater
> Than nobleness and riches,"

is like a first study for Prospero. In the fifth act, Marina, so named from her birth at sea, has grown to the age of fourteen years, and is, as it were, a sister of Miranda and Perdita (note in each case the significant name). She, like Perdita, is a child lost by her parents, and, like Perdita, we see her flower-like with her flowers—only these flowers of Marina are not for a merrymaking, but a grave. The melancholy of Pericles is a clear-obscure of sadness, not a gloom of cloudy remorse like that of Leontes. His meeting with his lost Marina is like an anticipation of the scene in which Cymbeline recovers his sons and daughter; but the scene in *Pericles* is filled with a rarer, keener passion of joy. And again, the marvellous meeting between Leontes and Hermione is anticipated by the union of Pericles and his Thaisa. Thus *Pericles*, containing the motives of much that was worked out more fully in later dramas, may be said to bear to the Romances* somewhat of the same relation which *The Two Gentlemen of Verona* bears to the comedies of love which succeeded it in Shakspere's second dramatic period.

*Under this head Dowden groups *Pericles*, *Cymbeline*, *The Tempest*, and *The Winter's Tale*. He says: "There is a romantic element about these plays. In all there is the same romantic incident of lost children recovered by those to whom they are dear. . . . In all there is a beautiful romantic background of sea or mountain. The dramas have a grave beauty, a sweet serenity, which seem to render the name 'comedies' inappropriate."

PERICLES, PRINCE OF TYRE.

DRAMATIS PERSONÆ.

ANTIOCHUS, king of Antioch.
PERICLES, prince of Tyre.
HELICANUS, } two lords of Tyre.
ESCANES, }
SIMONIDES, king of Pentapolis.
CLEON, governor of Tarsus.
LYSIMACHUS, governor of Mytilene.
CERIMON, a lord of Ephesus.
THALIARD, a lord of Antioch.
PHILEMON, servant to Cerimon.
LEONINE, servant to Dionyza.
Marshal.
A Pandar.
BOULT, his servant.

The Daughter of Antiochus.
DIONYZA, wife to Cleon
THAISA, daughter to Simonides.
MARINA, daughter to Pericles and Thaisa.
LYCHORIDA, nurse to Marina.
A Bawd.

Lords, Knights, Gentlemen, Sailors, Pirates, Fishermen, and Messengers.

DIANA.

GOWER, as Chorus.

SCENE: *Dispersedly in various countries.*

ANTIOCH.

ACT I.

Enter GOWER.

Before the Palace of Antioch.

To sing a song that old was sung,
From ashes ancient Gower is come,
Assuming man's infirmities,
To glad your ear and please your eyes.
It hath been sung at festivals,
On ember-eves and holy-ales;
And lords and ladies in their lives
Have read it for restoratives:
The purchase is to make men glorious;
Et bonum quo antiquius, eo melius.
If you, born in these latter times,
When wit 's more ripe, accept my rhymes,
And that to hear an old man sing
May to your wishes pleasure bring,
I life would wish, and that I might
Waste it for you, like taper-light.

This Antioch, then, Antiochus the Great
Built up, this city, for his chiefest seat;
The fairest in all Syria,—
I tell you what mine authors say.
This king unto him took a fere,
Who died and left a female heir,
So buxom, blithe, and full of face,
As heaven had lent her all his grace;
With whom the father liking took,
And her to incest did provoke.
Bad child, worse father! to entice his own
To evil should be done by none;
But custom what they did begin
Was with long use account no sin.
The beauty of this sinful dame
Made many princes thither frame,
To seek her as a bed-fellow,
In marriage-pleasures play-fellow;
Which to prevent he made a law,
To keep her still, and men in awe,
That whoso ask'd her for his wife,
His riddle told not, lost his life:
So for her many a wight did die,
As yon grim looks do testify.
What now ensues, to the judgment of your eye
I give, my cause who best can justify. [*Exit.*

SCENE I. *Antioch. A Room in the Palace.*

Enter ANTIOCHUS, PRINCE PERICLES, *and followers.*

Antiochus. Young prince of Tyre, you have at large receiv'd
The danger of the task you undertake.

Pericles. I have, Antiochus, and, with a soul
Embolden'd with the glory of her praise,
Think death no hazard in this enterprise.

Antiochus. Bring in our daughter, clothed like a bride,
For the embracements even of Jove himself;
At whose conception, till Lucina reign'd,
Nature this dowry gave, to glad her presence,—
The senate-house of planets all did sit,
To knit in her their best perfections.

Music. Enter the Daughter of Antiochus.

Pericles. See where she comes, apparell'd like the spring,
Graces her subjects, and her thoughts the king
Of every virtue gives renown to men!
Her face the book of praises, where is read
Nothing but curious pleasures, as from thence
Sorrow were ever raz'd, and testy wrath
Could never be her mild companion.
You gods that made me man, and sway in love,
That have inflam'd desire in my breast
To taste the fruits of yon celestial tree,
Or die in the adventure, be my helps,
As I am son and servant to your will,
To compass such a boundless happiness!

Antiochus. Prince Pericles,—

Pericles. That would be son to great Antiochus.

Antiochus. Before thee stands this fair Hesperides,
With golden fruit, but dangerous to be touch'd;
For death-like dragons here affright thee hard.
Her face, like heaven, enticeth thee to view
Her countless glory, which desert must gain;
And which, without desert, because thine eye
Presumes to reach, all thy whole heap must die.
Yon sometimes famous princes, like thyself,
Drawn by report, adventurous by desire,
Tell thee, with speechless tongues and semblance pale,
That without covering, save yon field of stars,
Here they stand martyrs, slain in Cupid's wars,
And with dead cheeks advise thee to desist
For going on death's net, whom none resist.

Pericles. Antiochus, I thank thee, who hath taught
My frail mortality to know itself,
And by those fearful objects to prepare
This body, like to them, to what I must;
For death remember'd should be like a mirror,
Who tells us life 's but breath, to trust it error.
I 'll make my will then, and, as sick men do
Who know the world, see heaven, but, feeling woe,
Gripe not at earthly joys as erst they did:
So I bequeath a happy peace to you

And all good men, as every prince should do;
My riches to the earth from whence they came,—
But my unspotted fire of love to you.—
[*To the daughter of Antiochus.*
Thus ready for the way of life or death,
I wait the sharpest blow, Antiochus.

Antiochus. Scorning advice, read the conclusion then;
Which read and not expounded, 't is decreed,
As these before thee thou thyself shalt bleed.

Daughter. Of all say'd yet, mayst thou prove prosperous!
Of all say'd yet, I wish thee happiness!

Pericles. Like a bold champion, I assume the lists,
Nor ask advice of any other thought
But faithfulness and courage.
[*He reads the riddle.*]
I am no viper, yet I feed
On mother's flesh which did me breed.
I sought a husband, in which labour
I found that kindness in a father.
He 's father, son, and husband mild;
I mother, wife, and yet his child.
How they may be, and yet in two,
As you will live, resolve it you.
Sharp physic is the last; but, O you powers
That give heaven countless eyes to view men's acts,
Why cloud they not their sights perpetually,
If this be true, which makes me pale to read it?—
Fair glass of light, I lov'd you, and could still,
[*Takes hold of the hand of the Princess*
Were not this glorious casket stor'd with ill:
But I must tell you, now my thoughts revolt;
For he 's no man on whom perfections wait
That, knowing sin within, will touch the gate.
You are a fair viol, and your sense the strings;
Who, finger'd to make man his lawful music,
Would draw heaven down, and all the gods, to hearken;
But, being play'd upon before your time,
Hell only danceth at so harsh a chime.
Good sooth, I care not for you.

Antiochus. Prince Pericles, touch not, upon thy life,
For that 's an article within our law,

As dangerous as the rest. Your time 's expir'd;
Either expound now, or receive your sentence.

Pericles. Great king,
Few love to hear the sins they love to act;
'T would braid yourself too near for me to tell it.
Who has a book of all that monarchs do,
He 's more secure to keep it shut than shown:
For vice repeated is like the wandering wind,
Blows dust in others' eyes, to spread itself;
And yet the end of all is bought thus dear,
The breath is gone, and the sore eyes see clear
To stop the air would hurt them. The blind mole casts
Copp'd hills towards heaven, to tell the earth is throng'd
By man's oppression; and the poor worm doth die for 't.
Kings are earth's gods; in vice their law 's their will;
And if Jove stray, who dares say Jove doth ill?
It is enough you know; and it is fit,
What being more known grows worse, to smother it.
All love the womb that their first being bred,
Then give my tongue like leave to love my head.

Antiochus. [*Aside*] Heaven, that I had thy head! he has found the meaning;
But I will gloze with him.—Young prince of Tyre,
Though by the tenour of our strict edict,
Your exposition misinterpreting,
We might proceed to cancel of your days,
Yet hope, succeeding from so fair a tree
As your fair self, doth tune us otherwise.
Forty days longer we do respite you;
If by which time our secret be undone,
This mercy shows we 'll joy in such a son:
And until then your entertain shall be
As doth befit our honour and your worth. [*Exeunt all but Pericles.*

Pericles. How courtesy would seem to cover sin,
When what is done is like an hypocrite,
The which is good in nothing but in sight!
If it be true that I interpret false,
Then were it certain you were not so bad
As with foul incest to abuse your soul;
Where now you 're both a father and a son,
By your untimely claspings with your child,
Which pleasure fits an husband, not a father;

And she an eater of her mother's flesh,
By the defiling of her parent's bed;
And both like serpents are, who though they feed
On sweetest flowers, yet they poison breed.
Antioch, farewell! for wisdom sees, those men
Blush not in actions blacker than the night
Will shun no course to keep them from the light.
One sin, I know, another doth provoke;
Murther 's as near to lust as flame to smoke:
Poison and treason are the hands of sin,
Ay, and the targets, to put off the shame.
Then, lest my life be cropp'd to keep you clear,
By flight I 'll shun the danger which I fear. [*Exit.*

Re-enter ANTIOCHUS.

Antiochus. He hath found the meaning, for the which we mean
To have his head.
He must not live to trumpet forth my infamy,
Nor tell the world Antiochus doth sin
In such a loathed manner;
And therefore instantly this prince must die,
For by his fall my honour must keep high.—
Who attends us there?

Enter THALIARD.

Thaliard. Doth your highness call?

Antiochus. Thaliard,
You are of our chamber, and our mind partakes
Her private actions to your secrecy;
And for your faithfulness we will advance you.
Thaliard, behold, here 's poison, and here 's gold;
We hate the prince of Tyre, and thou must kill him:
It fits thee not to ask the reason why,
Because we bid it. Say, is it done?

Thaliard. My lord,
'T is done.

Antiochus. Enough.—

Enter a Messenger.

Let your breath cool yourself, telling your haste.

Messenger. My lord, prince Pericles is fled. [*Exit*

Antiochus. As thou
Wilt live, fly after; and like an arrow shot
From a well-experienc'd archer hits the mark
His eye doth level at, so thou ne'er return
Unless thou say 'Prince Pericles is dead.'

Thaliard. My lord,
If I can get him within my pistol's length,
I 'll make him sure enough; so farewell to your highness.

Antiochus. Thaliard, adieu!—[*Exit Thaliard.*] Till Pericles be dead,
My heart can lend no succour to my head. [*Exit.*

SCENE II. *Tyre. A Room in the Palace.*

Enter PERICLES.

Pericles. [*To Lords without*] Let none disturb us.—Why should this change of thoughts,
The sad companion, dull-eyed melancholy,
Be my so us'd a guest as not an hour,
In the day's glorious walk, or peaceful night,
The tomb where grief should sleep, can breed me quiet?
Here pleasures court mine eyes, and mine eyes shun them,
And danger, which I fear'd, is at Antioch,
Whose arm seems far too short to hit me here;
Yet neither pleasure's art can joy my spirits,
Nor yet the other's distance comfort me.
Then it is thus: the passions of the mind,
That have their first conception by misdread,
Have after-nourishment and life by care;
And what was first but fear what might be done,
Grows elder now and cares it be not done.
And so with me: the great Antiochus,
'Gainst whom I am too little to contend,
Since he 's so great can make his will his act,
Will think me speaking, though I swear to silence;
Nor boots it me to say I honour him,
If he suspect I may dishonour him:
And what may make him blush in being known,
He 'll stop the course by which it might be known;
With hostile forces he 'll o'erspread the land,

And with the ostent of war will look so huge,
Amazement shall drive courage from the state,
Our men be vanquish'd ere they do resist,
And subjects punish'd that ne'er thought offence:
Which care of them, not pity of myself,
Who am no more but as the tops of trees,
Which fence the roots they grow by and defend them,
Makes both my body pine and soul to languish,
And punish that before that he would punish.

Enter HELICANUS, *with other* Lords.

1 *Lord.* Joy and all comfort in your sacred breast!

2 *Lord.* And keep your mind, till you return to us,
Peaceful and comfortable!

Helicanus. Peace, peace, and give experience tongue.
They do abuse the king that flatter him:
For flattery is the bellows blows up sin;
The thing the which is flatter'd, but a spark,
To which the blast gives heat and stronger glowing;
Whereas reproof, obedient and in order,
Fits kings, as they are men, for they may err.—
When Signior Sooth here doth proclaim a peace,
He flatters you, makes war upon your life.
Prince, pardon me, or strike me, if you please;
I cannot be much lower than my knees.

Pericles. All leave us else; but let your cares o'erlook
What shipping and what lading 's in our haven,
And then return to us.—[*Exeunt Lords.*] Helicanus, thou
Hast moved us: what seest thou in our looks?

Helicanus. An angry brow, dread lord.

Pericles. If there be such a dart in princes' frowns,
How durst thy tongue move anger to our face?

Helicanus. How dare the plants look up to heaven, from whence
They have their nourishment?

Pericles. Thou know'st I have power
To take thy life from thee.

Helicanus. [*Kneeling*] I have ground the axe myself;
Do you but strike the blow.

Pericles. Rise, prithee, rise,
Sit down; thou art no flatterer:

I thank thee for it; and heaven forbid
That kings should let their ears hear their faults hid!
Fit counsellor and servant for a prince,
Who by thy wisdom mak'st a prince thy servant,
What wouldst thou have me do?

Helicanus. To bear with patience
Such griefs as you yourself do lay upon yourself.

Pericles. Thou speak'st like a physician, Helicanus,
That minister'st a potion unto me
That thou wouldst tremble to receive thyself.
Attend me, then: I went to Antioch,
Where as thou know'st, against the face of death,
I sought the purchase of a glorious beauty,
From whence an issue I might propagate,
Are arms to princes, and bring joys to subjects.
Her face was to mine eye beyond all wonder,
The rest—hark in thine ear—as black as incest;
Which by my knowledge found, the sinful father
Seem'd not to strike, but smooth: but thou know'st this,
'T is time to fear when tyrants seem to kiss.
Which fear so grew in me, I hither fled,
Under the covering of a careful night,
Who seem'd my good protector; and, being here,
Bethought me what was past, what might succeed.
I knew him tyrannous; and tyrants' fears
Decrease not, but grow faster than the years:
And should he doubt it, as no doubt he doth,
That I should open to the listening air
How many worthy princes' bloods were shed,
To keep his bed of blackness unlaid ope,
To lop that doubt, he'll fill this land with arms,
And make pretence of wrong that I have done him;
When all, for mine—if I may call 't—offence,
Must feel war's blow, who spares not innocence;
Which love to all, of which thyself art one,
Who now reprov'st me for it,—

Helicanus. Alas, sir!

Pericles. Drew sleep out of mine eyes, blood from my cheeks,
Musings into my mind, with thousand doubts
How I might stop this tempest ere it came;

And finding little comfort to relieve them,
I thought it princely charity to grieve them.

Helicanus. Well, my lord, since you have given me leave to speak,
Freely will I speak. Antiochus you fear,
And justly too, I think, you fear the tyrant,
Who either by public war or private treason
Will take away your life.
Therefore, my lord, go travel for a while,
Till that his rage and anger be forgot,
Or till the Destinies do cut his thread of life.
Your rule direct to any; if to me,
Day serves not light more faithful than I 'll be.

Pericles. I do not doubt thy faith;
But should he wrong my liberties in my absence?

Helicanus. We 'll mingle our bloods together in the earth,
From whence we had our being and our birth.

Pericles. Tyre, I now look from thee then, and to Tarsus
Intend my travel, where I 'll hear from thee;
And by whose letters I 'll dispose myself.
The care I had and have of subjects' good
On thee I lay, whose wisdom's strength can bear it.
I 'll take thy word for faith, not ask thine oath;
Who shuns not to break one will sure crack both.
But in our orbs we 'll live so round and safe,
That time of both this truth shall ne'er convince,—
Thou show'dst a subject's shine, I a true prince. [*Exeunt.*

SCENE III. *Tyre. An Ante-chamber in the Palace.*

Enter THALIARD.

Thaliard. So, this is Tyre, and this the court. Here must I kill King Pericles; and if I do it not, I am sure to be hanged at home: 't is dangerous.—Well, I perceive he was a wise fellow and had good discretion, that, being bid to ask what he would of the king, desired he might know none of his secrets: now do I see he had some reason for 't; for if a king bid a man be a villain, he 's bound by the indenture of his oath to be one.—Hush! here come the lords of Tyre.

Enter HELICANUS, ESCANES, *and other* Lords.

Helicanus. You shall not need, my fellow peers of Tyre,

Further to question me of your king's departure;
His seal'd commission, left in trust with me,
Doth speak sufficiently he 's gone to travel.

Thaliard. [*Aside*] How! the king gone!

Helicanus. If further yet you will be satisfied,
Why, as it were unlicens'd of your loves,
He would depart, I 'll give some light unto you.
Being at Antioch—

Thaliard. [*Aside*] What from Antioch?

Helicanus. Royal Antiochus—on what cause I know not—
Took some displeasure at him; at least he judg'd so:
And doubting lest that he had err'd or sinn'd,
To show his sorrow, he 'd correct himself:
So puts himself unto the shipman's toil,
With whom each minute threatens life or death.

Thaliard. [*Aside*] Well, I perceive
I shall not be hang'd now, although I would;
But since he 's gone, the king's ears it must please:
He scap'd the land, to perish at the sea.
I 'll present myself.—Peace to the lords of Tyre!

Helicanus. Lord Thaliard from Antiochus is welcome.

Thaliard. From him I come
With message unto princely Pericles;
But since my landing I have understood
Your lord has betook himself to unknown travels,
My message must return from whence it came.

Helicanus. We have no reason to desire it,
Commended to our master, not to us;
Yet, ere you shall depart, this we desire,
As friends to Antioch, we may feast in Tyre. [*Exeunt*

SCENE IV. *Tarsus. A Room in the Governor's House.*

Enter CLEON, DIONYZA, *and* Attendants.

Cleon. My Dionyza, shall we rest us here,
And by relating tales of others' griefs,
See if 't will teach us to forget our own?

Dionyza. That were to blow at fire in hope to quench it;
For who digs hills because they do aspire
Throws down one mountain to cast up a higher.

O my distressed lord, even such our griefs;
Here they 're but felt, and seen with mischief's eyes,
But like to groves, being topp'd, they higher rise.

Cleon. O Dionyza,
Who wanteth food, and will not say he wants it,
Or can conceal his hunger till he famish?
Our tongues and sorrows do sound deep
Our woes into the air; our eyes do weep
Till tongues fetch breath that may proclaim them louder;
That, if heaven slumber while their creatures want,
They may awake their helps to comfort them.
I 'll then discourse our woes, felt several years,
And wanting breath to speak, help me with tears.

Dionyza. I 'll do my best, sir.

Cleon. This Tarsus, o'er which I have the government,
A city on whom plenty held full hand,
For riches strew'd herself even in the streets;
Whose towers bore heads so high they kiss'd the clouds,
And strangers ne'er beheld but wonder'd at;
Whose men and dames so jetted and adorn'd,
Like one another's glass to trim them by:
Their tables were stor'd full, to glad the sight,
And not so much to feed on as delight;
All poverty was scorn'd, and pride so great,
The name of help grew odious to repeat.

Dionyza. O, 't is too true.

Cleon. But see what heaven can do! By this our change,
These mouths, who but of late earth, sea, and air,
Were all too little to content and please,
Although they gave their creatures in abundance,
As houses are defil'd for want of use,
They are now starv'd for want of exercise;
Those palates who, not yet two summers younger,
Must have inventions to delight the taste,
Would now be glad of bread, and beg for it;
Those mothers who, to nousle up their babes,
Thought nought too curious, are ready now
To eat those little darlings whom they lov'd.
So sharp are hunger's teeth, that man and wife
Draw lots who first shall die to lengthen life:
Here stands a lord, and there a lady weeping;

Here many sink, yet those which see them fall
Have scarce strength left to give them burial.
Is not this true?

Dionyza. Our cheeks and hollow eyes do witness it.

Cleon. O, let those cities that of plenty's cup
And her prosperities so largely taste,
With their superfluous riots, hear these tears!
The misery of Tarsus may be theirs.

Enter a Lord.

Lord. Where's the lord governor?

Cleon. Here.
Speak out thy sorrows which thou bring'st in haste,
For comfort is too far for us to expect.

Lord. We have descried, upon our neighbouring shore,
A portly sail of ships make hitherward.

Cleon. I thought as much.
One sorrow never comes but brings an heir,
That may succeed as his inheritor;
And so in ours. Some neighbouring nation,
Taking advantage of our misery,
Hath stuff'd these hollow vessels with their power,
To beat us down, the which are down already,
And make a conquest of unhappy me,
Whereas no glory's got to overcome.

Lord. That's the least fear; for, by the semblance
Of their white flags display'd, they bring us peace,
And come to us as favourers, not as foes.

Cleon. Thou speak'st like him's untutor'd to repeat;
Who makes the fairest show means most deceit.
But bring they what they will and what they can,
What need we fear?
The ground's the lowest, and we are half way there.
Go tell their general we attend him here,
To know for what he comes, and whence he comes,
And what he craves.

Lord. I go, my lord. [*Exit.*

Cleon. Welcome is peace, if he on peace consist;
If wars, we are unable to resist.

Enter PERICLES *with* Attendants.

Pericles. Lord governor, for so we hear you are,
Let not our ships and number of our men
Be like a beacon fir'd to amaze your eyes.
We have heard your miseries as far as Tyre,
And seen the desolation of your streets:
Nor come we to add sorrow to your tears,
But to relieve them of their heavy load;
And these our ships, you happily may think
Are like the Trojan horse was stuff'd within
With bloody veins, expecting overthrow,
Are stor'd with corn to make your needy bread,
And give them life whom hunger starv'd half dead.

All. The gods of Greece protect you!
And we 'll pray for you.

Pericles. Arise, I pray you, rise;
We do not look for reverence, but for love,
And harbourage for ourself, our ships, and men.

Cleon. The which when any shall not gratify,
Or pay you with unthankfulness in thought,
Be it our wives, our children, or ourselves,
The curse of heaven and men succeed their evils!
Till when—the which I hope shall ne'er be seen—
Your grace is welcome to our town and us.

Pericles. Which welcome we 'll accept; feast here awhile,
Until our stars that frown lend us a smile. [*Exeunt*

ACT II.

Enter GOWER.

Gower. Here have you seen a mighty king
His child, I wis, to incest bring;
A better prince and benign lord,
That will prove awful both in deed and word.
Be quiet then as men should be,
Till he hath pass'd necessity.

I 'll show you those in troubles reign,
Losing a mite, a mountain gain.
The good in conversation,
To whom I give my benison,
Is still at Tarsus, where each man
Thinks all is writ he speken can,
And, to remember what he does,
Build his statue to make him glorious;
But tidings to the contrary
Are brought your eyes,—what need speak I?

Dumb Show.

Enter at one door Pericles *talking with* Cleon; *all the train with them. Enter at another door a* Gentleman, *with a letter to* Pericles; Pericles *shows the letter to* Cleon; *gives the* Messenger *a reward, and knights him. Exit* Pericles *at one door, and* Cleon *at another.*

Good Helicane, that stay'd at home—
Not to eat honey like a drone
From others' labours, though he strive
To killen bad, keep good alive,
And to fulfil his prince' desire—
Sends word of all that haps in Tyre:
How Thaliard came full bent with sin
And had intent to murther him;
And that in Tarsus was not best
Longer for him to make his rest.
He, doing so, put forth to seas,
Where when men been, there 's seldom ease:
For now the wind begins to blow;
Thunder above and deeps below
Make such unquiet, that the ship
Should house him safe is wrack'd and split;
And he, good prince, having all lost,
By waves from coast to coast is tost.
All perishen of man, of pelf,
Ne aught escapen but himself;
Till fortune, tir'd with doing bad,
Threw him ashore, to give him glad:
And here he comes. What shall be next,
Pardon old Gower,—this longs the text. *Exit.*

SCENE I. *Pentapolis. An open Place by the Seaside.*

Enter PERICLES, *wet.*

Pericles. Yet cease your ire, you angry stars of heaven!
Wind, rain, and thunder, remember, earthly man
Is but a substance that must yield to you;
And I, as fits my nature, do obey you.
Alas, the sea hath cast me on the rocks,
Wash'd me from shore to shore, and left me breath
Nothing to think on but ensuing death.
Let it suffice the greatness of your powers
To have bereft a prince of all his fortunes;
And having thrown him from your watery grave,
Here to have death in peace is all he 'll crave.

Enter three Fishermen.

1 *Fisherman.* What, ho, Pilch!

2 *Fisherman.* Ha, come and bring away the nets!

1 *Fisherman.* What, Patch-breech, I say!

3 *Fisherman.* What say you, master?

1 *Fisherman.* Look how thou stirrest now! come away, or I 'll fetch thee with a wanion.

3 *Fisherman.* Faith, master, I am thinking of the poor men that were cast away before us even now.

1 *Fisherman.* Alas, poor souls, it grieved my heart to hear what pitiful cries they made to us to help them, when, well-a-day, we could scarce help ourselves.

3 *Fisherman.* Nay, master, said not I as much when I saw the porpus how he bounced and tumbled? they say they 're half fish, half flesh; a plague on them, they ne'er come but I look to be washed. Master, I marvel how the fishes live in the sea.

1 *Fisherman.* Why, as men do a-land; the great ones eat up the little ones. I can compare our rich misers to nothing so fitly as to a whale; a' plays and tumbles, driving the poor fry before him, and at last devours them all at a mouthful. Such whales have I heard on o' the land, who never leave gaping till they 've swallowed the whole parish, church, steeple, bells, and all.

Pericles. [*Aside*] A pretty moral.

3 *Fisherman*. But, master, if I had been the sexton, I would have been that day in the belfry.

2 *Fisherman*. Why, man?

3 *Fisherman*. Because he should have swallowed me too; and when I had been in his belly, I would have kept such a jangling of the bells, that he should never have left till he cast bells, steeple, church, and parish, up again. But if the good King Simonides were of my mind,—

Pericles. [*Aside*] Simonides!

3 *Fisherman*. We would purge the land of these drones, that rob the bee of her honey.

Pericles. [*Aside*] How from the finny subject of the sea
These fishers tell the infirmities of men,
And from their watery empire recollect
All that may men approve or men detect!—
Peace be at your labour, honest fishermen.

2 *Fisherman*. Honest! good fellow, what 's that? If it be a day fits you, search out of the calendar, and nobody look after it.

Pericles. You may see the sea hath cast me on your coast.

2 *Fisherman*. What a drunken knave was the sea to cast thee in our way!

Pericles. A man whom both the waters and the wind,
In that vast tennis-court, hath made the ball
For them to play upon, entreats you pity him;
He asks of you, that never us'd to beg.

1 *Fisherman*. No, friend, cannot you beg? Here 's them in our country of Greece gets more with begging than we can do with working.

2 *Fisherman*. Canst thou catch any fishes then?

Pericles. I never practis'd it.

2 *Fisherman*. Nay, then thou wilt starve, sure; for here 's nothing to be got now-a-days, unless thou canst fish for 't.

Pericles. What I have been I have forgot to know,
But what I am want teaches me to think on,—
A man throng'd up with cold: my veins are chill,
And have no more of life than may suffice
To give my tongue that heat to ask your help;
Which if you shall refuse, when I am dead,
For that I am a man, pray see me buried.

1 *Fisherman*. Die, quoth-a? Now gods forbid! I have a gown here; come, put it on; keep thee warm. Now, afore me, a handsome

fellow! Come, thou shalt go home, and we 'll have flesh for holidays, fish for fasting-days, and moreo'er puddings and flap-jacks, and thou shalt be welcome.

Pericles. I thank you, sir.

2 *Fisherman.* Hark you, my friend; you said you could not beg.

Pericles. I did but crave.

2 *Fisherman.* But crave! Then I will turn craver too, and so I shall scape whipping.

Pericles. Why, are all your beggars whipped then?

2 *Fisherman.* O, not all, my friend, not all; for if all your beggars were whipped, I would wish no better office than to be beadle.—But, master, I 'll go draw up the net. [*Exeunt with Third Fisherman.*

Pericles. [*Aside*] How well this honest mirth becomes their labour!

1 *Fisherman.* Hark you, sir, do you know where ye are?

Pericles. Not well.

1 *Fisherman.* Why, I 'll tell you: this is called Pentapolis, and our king the good Simonides.

Pericles. The good King Simonides, do you call him?

1 *Fisherman.* Ay, sir; and he deserves so to be called for his peaceable reign and good government.

Pericles. He is a happy king, since he gains from his subjects the name of good by his government. How far is his court distant from this shore?

1 *Fisherman.* Marry, sir, half a day's journey: and I 'll tell you, he hath a fair daughter, and to-morrow is her birth-day; and there are princes and knights come from all parts of the world to just and tourney for her love.

Pericles. Were my fortunes equal to my desires, I could wish to make one there.

1 *Fisherman.* O, sir, things must be as they may; and what a man cannot get, he may lawfully deal for . . . his wife's soul.

Re-enter Second and Third Fisherman, drawing up a net.

2 *Fisherman.* Help, master, help! here 's a fish hangs in the net, like a poor man's right in the law; 't will hardly come out. Ha! bots on 't, 't is come at last, and 't is turned to a rusty armour.

Pericles. An armour, friends! I pray you, let me see it.
Thanks, fortune, yet, that, after all thy crosses,

Thou giv'st me somewhat to repair myself;
And though it was mine own, part of my heritage,
Which my dead father did bequeath to me,
With this strict charge, even as he left his life,
'Keep it, my Pericles; it hath been a shield
'Twixt me and death;'—and pointed to this brace—
'For that it sav'd me, keep it; in like necessity—
The which the gods protect thee from!—'t may defend thee.'
It kept where I kept, I so dearly lov'd it;
Till the rough seas, that spare not any man,
Took it in rage, though calm'd have given 't again.
I thank thee for 't; my shipwrack now 's no ill,
Since I have here my father's gift in 's will.

1 *Fisherman.* What mean you, sir?

Pericles. To beg of you, kind friends, this coat of worth
For it was sometime target to a king;
I know it by this mark. He lov'd me dearly,
And for his sake I wish the having of it;
And that you 'd guide me to your sovereign's court,
Where with it I may appear a gentleman:
And if that ever my low fortune 's better,
I 'll pay your bounties; till then rest your debtor.

1 *Fisherman.* Why, wilt thou tourney for the lady?

Pericles. I 'll show the virtue I have borne in arms.

1 *Fisherman.* Why, do 'e take it, and the gods give thee good on 't!

2 *Fisherman.* Ay, but hark you, my friend; 't was we that made up this garment through the rough seams of the waters: there are certain condolements, certain vails. I hope, sir, if you thrive, you 'll remember from whence you had it.

Pericles. Believe 't, I will.
By your furtherance I am clothed in steel;
And, spite of all the rapture of the sea,
This jewel holds his building on my arm.
Unto thy value I will mount myself
Upon a courser, whose delightful steps
Shall make the gazer joy to see him tread.
Only, my friend, I yet am unprovided
Of a pair of bases.

2 *Fisherman.* We 'll sure provide: thou shalt have my best gown to make thee a pair; and I 'll bring thee to the court myself.

Pericles. Then honour be but a goal to my will,
This day I 'll rise, or else add ill to ill. [*Exeunt.*

SCENE II. *The Same. A Platform leading to the Lists. A Pavilion near it for the reception of the King, Princess, Lords, etc.*

Enter SIMONIDES, THAISA, Lords, *and* Attendants.

Simonides. Are the knights ready to begin the triumph?

1 *Lord.* They are, my liege,
And stay your coming to present themselves.

Simonides. Return them, we are ready; and our daughter,
In honour of whose birth these triumphs are,
Sits here, like beauty's child, whom nature gat
For men to see, and seeing wonder at. [*Exit a Lord.*

Thaisa. It pleaseth you, my royal father, to express
My commendations great, whose merit 's less.

Simonides. It 's fit it should be so; for princes are
A model which heaven makes like to itself.
As jewels lose their glory if neglected,
So princes their renowns if not respected.
'T is now your honour, daughter, to interpret
The labour of each knight in his device.

Thaisa. Which, to preserve mine honour, I 'll perform.

Enter a Knight; *he passes over, and his* Squire *presents his shield to the* Princess.

Simonides. Who is the first that doth prefer himself?

Thaisa. A knight of Sparta, my renowned father,
And the device he bears upon his shield
Is a black Ethiope reaching at the sun;
The word, 'Lux tua vita mihi.'

Simonides. He loves you well that holds his life for you.
[*The Second Knight passes over.*
Who is the second that presents himself?

Thaisa. A prince of Macedon, my royal father,
And the device he bears upon his shield

Is an arm'd knight that 's conquer'd by a lady;
The motto thus, in Spanish, 'Piu por dulzura que por fuerza.'
[*The Third Knight passes over.*

Simonides. And what 's the third?

Thaisa. The third of Antioch,
And his device, a wreath of chivalry;
The word, 'Me pompae provexit apex.'
[*The Fourth Knight passes over.*

Simonides. What is the fourth?

Thaisa. A burning torch that 's turned upside down;
The word, 'Quod me alit, me extinguit.'

Simonides. Which shows that beauty hath his power and will,
Which can as well inflame as it can kill.
[*The Fifth Knight passes over.*

Thaisa. The fifth, an hand environed with clouds,
Holding out gold that 's by the touchstone tried;
The motto thus, 'Sic spectanda fides.'
[*The Sixth Knight, Pericles, passes over.*

Simonides. And what 's
The sixth and last, the which the knight himself
With such a graceful courtesy deliver'd?

Thaisa. He seems to be a stranger, but his present is
A wither'd branch, that 's only green at top;
The motto, 'In hac spe vivo.'

Simonides. A pretty moral;
From the dejected state wherein he is,
He hopes by you his fortunes yet may flourish.

1 *Lord.* He had need mean better than his outward show
Can any way speak in his just commend;
For by his rusty outside he appears
To have practis'd more the whipstock than the lance.

2 *Lord.* He well may be a stranger, for he comes
To an honour'd triumph strangely furnished.

3 *Lord.* And on set purpose let his armour rust
Until this day, to scour it in the dust.

Simonides. Opinion 's but a fool, that makes us scan
The outward habit by the inward man.
But stay, the knights are coming; we will withdraw
Into the gallery. [*Exeunt.*

[*Great shouts within, and all cry* 'The mean knight!'

SCENE III. *The Same. A Hall of State: a Banquet prepared.*

Enter SIMONIDES, THAISA, Lords, Knights, and Attendants.

Simonides. Knights,
To say you 're welcome were superfluous.
To place upon the volume of your deeds,
As in a title-page, your worth in arms,
Were more than you expect, or more than 's fit,
Since every worth in show commends itself.
Prepare for mirth, for mirth becomes a feast;
You are princes and my guests.

Thaisa. But you, my knight and guest,
To whom this wreath of victory I give,
And crown you king of this day's happiness.

Pericles. 'T is more by fortune, lady, than by merit.

Simonides. Call it by what you will, the day is yours;
And here, I hope, is none that envies it.
In framing an artist, art hath thus decreed,
To make some good, but others to exceed;
And you are her labour'd scholar.—Come, queen o' the feast,—
For, daughter, so you are,—here take your place;
Marshal the rest, as they deserve their grace.

Knights. We are honour'd much by good Simonides.

Simonides. Your presence glads our days; honour we love,
For who hates honour hates the gods above.

Marshal. Sir, yonder is your place.

Pericles. Some other is more fit.

1 *Knight.* Contend not, sir; for we are gentlemen
That neither in our hearts nor outward eyes
Envy the great nor do the low despise.

Pericles. You are right courteous knights.

Simonides. Sit, sir, sit.—
By Jove, I wonder, that is king of thoughts,
These cates resist me, he not thought upon.

Thaisa. By Juno, that is queen of marriage.
All viands that I eat do seem unsavoury,
Wishing him my meat.—Sure, he 's a gallant gentleman.

Simonides. He 's but a country gentleman,
Has done no more than other knights have done,
Has broken a staff or so; so let it pass.

Thaisa. To me he seems like diamond to glass.

Pericles. Yon king 's to me like to my father's picture,
Which tells me in that glory once he was;
Had princes sit, like stars, about his throne,
And he the sun, for them to reverence.
None that beheld him but, like lesser lights,
Did vail their crowns to his supremacy;
Where now his son 's like a glow-worm in the night,
The which hath fire in darkness, none in light:
Whereby I see that Time 's the king of men;
For he 's their parent, and he is their grave,
And gives them what he will, not what they crave.

Simonides. What, are you merry, knights?

Knights. Who can be other in this royal presence?

Simonides. Here, with a cup that 's stor'd unto the brim,—
As you do love, fill to your mistress' lips,—
We drink this health to you.

Knights. We thank your grace.

Simonides. Yet pause awhile;
Yon knight doth sit too melancholy,
As if the entertainment in our court
Had not a show might countervail his worth.—
Note it not you, Thaisa?

Thaisa. What is it
To me, my father?

Simonides. O, attend, my daughter:
Princes in this should live like gods above,
Who freely give to every one that comes
To honour them;
And princes not doing so are like to gnats,
Which make a sound, but kill'd are wonder'd at.
Therefore to make his entrance more sweet,
Here, say we drink this standing-bowl of wine to him.

Thaisa. Alas, my father, it befits not me
Unto a stranger knight to be so bold.
He may my proffer take for an offence,
Since men take women's gifts for impudence.

Simonides. How?
Do as I bid you, or you 'll move me else.
Thaisa. [*Aside*] Now, by the gods, he could not please me better
Simonides. And furthermore tell him, we desire to know of him,
Of whence he is, his name and parentage.
Thaisa. The king my father, sir, has drunk to you.
Pericles. I thank him.
Thaisa. Wishing it so much blood unto your life.
Pericles. I thank both him and you, and pledge him freely.
Thaisa. And further he desires to know of you,
Of whence you are, your name and parentage.
Pericles. A gentleman of Tyre; my name, Pericles;
My education been in arts and arms;
Who, looking for adventures in the world,
Was by the rough seas reft of ships and men,
And after shipwrack driven upon this shore.
Thaisa. He thanks your grace, names himself Pericles,
A gentleman of Tyre,
Who only by misfortune of the seas
Bereft of ships and men, cast on this shore.
Simonides. Now, by the gods, I pity his misfortune,
And will awake him from his melancholy.—
Come, gentlemen, we sit too long on trifles,
And waste the time, which looks for other revels.
Even in your armours, as you are address'd,
Will very well become a soldier's dance.
I will not have excuse, with saying this
Loud music is too harsh for ladies' heads,
Since they love men in arms as well as beds.— [*The Knights dance.*
So, this was well ask'd, 't was so well perform'd.—
Come, sir;
Here is a lady that wants breathing too:
And I have heard, you knights of Tyre
Are excellent in making ladies trip,
And that their measures are as excellent.
Pericles. In those that practise them they are, my lord.
Simonides. O, that 's as much as you would be denied
Of your fair courtesy.— [*The Knights and Ladies dance.*
Unclasp, unclasp:

Thanks, gentlemen, to all; all have done well,—
[*To Pericles*] But you the best.—Pages and lights, to conduct
These knights unto their several lodgings!—[*To Pericles*] Yours, sir,
We have given order to be next our own.

Pericles. I am at your grace's pleasure.

Simonides. Princes, it is too late to talk of love,
And that 's the mark I know you level at:
Therefore each one betake him to his rest;
To-morrow all for speeding do their best. [*Exeunt.*

SCENE IV. *Tyre. A Room in the Governor's House.*

Enter HELICANUS *and* ESCANES.

Helicanus. No, Escanes, know this of me,
Antiochus from incest liv'd not free:
For which the most high gods not minding longer
To withhold the vengeance that they had in store,
Due to the heinous capital offence,
Even in the height and pride of all his glory,
When he was seated in a chariot
Of an inestimable value, and his daughter with him,
A fire from heaven came and shrivell'd up
Their bodies, even to loathing; for they so stunk,
That all those eyes ador'd them ere their fall
Scorn now their hand should give them burial.

Escanes. 'T was very strange.

Helicanus. And yet but justice; for though
This king were great, his greatness was no guard
To bar heaven's shaft, but sin had his reward.

Escanes. 'T is very true.

Enter two or three Lords.

1 *Lord.* See, not a man in private conference
Or council has respect with him but he.

2 *Lord.* It shall no longer grieve without reproof.

3 *Lord.* And curs'd be he that will not second it.

1 *Lord.* Follow me, then.—Lord Helicane, a word.

Helicanus. With me? and welcome.—Happy day, my lords.

1 *Lord.* Know that our griefs are risen to the top,
And now at length they overflow their banks.

Helicanus. Your griefs! for what? wrong not your prince you love.

1 *Lord.* Wrong not yourself, then, noble Helicane;
But if the prince do live, let us salute him,
Or know what ground 's made happy by his breath.
If in the world he live, we 'll seek him out;
If in his grave he rest, we 'll find him there,
And be resolv'd he lives to govern us,
Or, dead, gives cause to mourn his funeral,
And leave us to our free election.

2 *Lord.* Whose death indeed 's the strongest in our censure;
And knowing this kingdom is without a head,—
Like goodly buildings left without a roof
Soon fall to ruin,—your noble self,
That best know how to rule and how to reign,
We thus submit unto,—our sovereign.

All. Live, noble Helicane!

Helicanus. For honour's cause, forbear your suffrages;
If that you love Prince Pericles, forbear.
Take I your wish, I leap into the seas,
Where 's hourly trouble for a minute's ease.
A twelvemonth longer, let me entreat you
To forbear the absence of your king;
If in which time expir'd he not return,
I shall with aged patience bear your yoke.
But if I cannot win you to this love,
Go search like nobles, like noble subjects,
And in your search spend your adventurous worth;
Whom if you find, and win unto return,
You shall like diamonds sit about his crown.

1 *Lord.* To wisdom he 's a fool that will not yield;
And since Lord Helicane enjoineth us,
We with our travels will endeavour it.

Helicanus. Then you love us, we you, and we 'll clasp hands;
When peers thus knit, a kingdom ever stands. [*Exeunt.*

SCENE V. *Pentapolis. A Room in the Palace.*

Enter SIMONIDES, *reading a letter; the* Knights *meet him.*

1 *Knight.* Good morrow to the good Simonides.

Simonides. Knights, from my daughter this I let you know,
That for this twelvemonth she 'll not undertake
A married life.
Her reason to herself is only known,
Which yet from her by no means can I get.

2 *Knight.* May we not get access to her, my lord?

Simonides. Faith, by no means; she hath so strictly tied
Her to her chamber, that 't is impossible.
One twelve moons more she 'll wear Diana's livery;
This by the eye of Cynthia hath she vow'd,
And on her virgin honour will not break it.

3 *Knight.* Loath to bid farewell, we take our leaves.
[*Exeunt Knights.*

Simonides. So,
They are well dispatch'd; now to my daughter's letter.
She tells me here, she 'll wed the stranger knight,
Or never more to view nor day nor light.
'T is well, mistress; your choice agrees with mine;
I like that well: nay, how absolute she 's in 't,
Not minding whether I dislike or no!
Well, I do commend her choice,
And will no longer have it be delay'd.—
Soft! here he comes; I must dissemble it.

Enter PERICLES.

Pericles. All fortune to the good Simonides!

Simonides. To you as much, sir! I am beholding to you
For your sweet music this last night; I do
Protest, my ears were never better fed
With such delightful pleasing harmony.

Pericles. It is your grace's pleasure to commend,
Not my desert.

Simonides. Sir, you are music's master.

Pericles. The worst of all her scholars, my good lord.

Simonides. Let me ask you one thing :
What do you think of my daughter, sir.
Pericles. A most virtuous princess.
Simonides. And she is fair too, is she not?
Pericles. As a fair day in summer, wondrous fair.
Simonides. Sir, my daughter thinks very well of you;
Ay, so well, that you must be her master,
And she will be your scholar: therefore look to it.
Pericles. I am unworthy for her schoolmaster.
Simonides. She thinks not so; peruse this writing else.
Pericles. [*Aside*] What 's here?
A letter that she loves the knight of Tyre!
'T is the king's subtilty to have my life.—
O, seek not to entrap me, gracious lord,
A stranger and distressed gentleman,
That never aim'd so high to love your daughter,
But bent all offices to honour her.
Simonides. Thou hast bewitch'd my daughter, and thou art
A villain.
Pericles. By the gods, I have not;
Never did thought of mine levy offence,
Nor never did my actions yet commence
A deed might gain her love or your displeasure.
Simonides. Traitor, thou liest.
Pericles. Traitor!
Simonides. Ay, traitor.
Pericles. Even in his throat—unless it be the king—
That calls me traitor, I return the lie.
Simonides. [*Aside*] Now, by the gods, I do applaud his courage.
Pericles. My actions are as noble as my thoughts,
That never relish'd of a base descent.
I came unto your court for honour's cause,
And not to be a rebel to her state;
And he that otherwise accounts of me,
This sword shall prove he 's honour's enemy.
Simonides. No?—
Here comes my daughter, she can witness it.

Enter THAISA.

Pericles. Then, as you are as virtuous as fair,
Resolve your angry father, if my tongue
Did e'er solicit, or my hand subscribe
To any syllable that made love to you.
Thaisa. Why, sir, say if you had,
Who takes offence at that would make me glad?
Simonides. Yea, mistress, are you so peremptory?—
[*Aside*] I am glad on 't with all my heart.—
I 'll tame you; I 'll bring you in subjection.
Will you, not having my consent,
Bestow your love and your affections
Upon a stranger? [*aside*] who, for aught I know,
May be, nor can I think the contrary,
As great in blood as I myself.—
Therefore hear you, mistress; either frame
Your will to mine,—and you, sir, hear you,
Either be rul'd by me, or I will make you—
Man and wife.—
Nay, come, your hands and lips must seal it too:
And being join'd, I 'll thus your hopes destroy;
And for a further grief,—God give you joy!—
What, are you both pleas'd?
Thaisa. Yes, if you love me, sir.
Pericles. Even as my life, or blood that fosters it.
Simonides. What, are you both agreed?
Both. Yes, if it please your majesty.
Simonides. It pleaseth me so well, that I will see you wed;
And then, with what haste you can, get you to bed. [*Exeunt.*

ACT III.

Enter GOWER.

Gower. Now sleep yslaked hath the rout;
No din but snores the house about,
Made louder by the o'er-fed breast
Of this most pompous marriage-feast.
The cat, with eyne of burning coal,
Now couches fore the mouse's hole;
And crickets sing at the oven's mouth,
E'er the blither for their drouth.
Hymen hath brought the bride to bed,
Where, by the loss of maidenhead,
A babe is moulded. Be attent,
And time that is so briefly spent
With your fine fancies quaintly eche;
What 's dumb in show I'll plain with speech.

DUMB SHOW.

Enter PERICLES *and* SIMONIDES, *with* Attendants; *a* Messenger *meets them, kneels, and gives* PERICLES *a letter;* PERICLES *shows it* SIMONIDES; *the* Lords *kneel to him. Then enter* THAISA *with child, and* LYCHORIDA. *The* KING *shows his daughter the letter; she rejoices: she and* PERICLES *take leave of her father, and depart with* LYCHORIDA *and their* Attendants. *Then exeunt* SIMONIDES *and the rest.*

By many a dern and painful perch
Of Pericles the careful search,
By the four opposing coigns
Which the world together joins,
Is made with all due diligence
That horse and sail and high expense
Can stead the quest. At last from Tyre,
Fame answering the most strange inquire,
To the court of King Simonides
Are letters brought, the tenour these:
Antiochus and his daughter dead;
The men of Tyrus on the head
Of Helicanus would set on
The crown of Tyre, but he will none;
The mutiny he there hastes t' oppress;
Says to 'em, if King Pericles
Come not home in twice six moons,
He, obedient to their dooms,
Will take the crown. The sum of this,
Brought hither to Pentapolis,
Yravished the regions round,
And every one with claps can sound,
'Our heir-apparent is a king!
Who dream'd, who thought of such a thing?'
Brief, he must hence depart to Tyre;
His queen with child makes her desire—
Which who shall cross?—along to go.
Omit we all their dole and woe;
Lychorida, her nurse, she takes,
And so to sea. Their vessel shakes
On Neptune's billow; half the flood
Hath their keel cut: but fortune's mood

Varies again; the grisly north
Disgorges such a tempest forth,
That, as a duck for life that dives,
So up and down the poor ship drives.
The lady shrieks, and well-a-near
Does fall in travail with her fear;
And what ensues in this fell storm
Shall for itself itself perform.
I nill relate, action may
Conveniently the rest convey;
Which might not what by me is told.
In your imagination hold
This stage the ship, upon whose deck
The sea-tost Pericles appears to speak. [*Exit.*

Scene I.

Enter Pericles, *on shipboard.*

Pericles. Thou god of this great vast, rebuke these surges,
Which wash both heaven and hell; and thou, that hast
Upon the winds command, bind them in brass,
Having call'd them from the deep! O, still
Thy deafening, dreadful thunders; gently quench
Thy nimble, sulphurous flashes!—O, how, Lychorida,
How does my queen?—Thou stormest venomously;
Wilt thou spet all thyself? The seaman's whistle
Is as a whisper in the ears of death,
Unheard.—Lychorida!—Lucina, O
Divinest patroness, and midwife gentle
To those that cry by night, convey thy deity
Aboard our dancing boat; make swift the pangs
Of my queen's travail!—

Enter Lychorida, *with an Infant.*

Now, Lychorida!

Lychorida. Here is a thing too young for such a place,
Who, if it had conceit, would die, as I

Am like to do. Take in your arms this piece
Of your dead queen.

Pericles. How, how, Lychorida!

Lychorida. Patience, good sir; do not assist the storm.
Here 's all that is left living of your queen,
A little daughter; for the sake of it,
Be manly, and take comfort.

Pericles. O you gods!
Why do you make us love your goodly gifts,
And snatch them straight away? We here below
Recall not what we give, and therein may
Vie honour with you.

Lychorida. Patience, good sir,
Even for this charge.

Pericles. Now, mild may be thy life!
For a more boisterous birth had never babe;
Quiet and gentle thy conditions! for
Thou art the rudeliest welcome to this world
That ever was prince's child. Happy what follows!
Thou hast as chiding a nativity
As fire, air, water, earth, and heaven can make,
To herald thee from the womb; even at the first
Thy loss is more than can thy portage quit,
With all thou canst find here.—Now, the good gods
Throw their best eyes upon 't!

Enter two Sailors.

1 *Sailor.* What courage, sir? God save you!

Pericles. Courage enough: I do not fear the flaw;
It hath done to me the worst. Yet, for the love
Of this poor infant, this fresh-new sea-farer,
I would it would be quiet.

1 *Sailor.* Slack the bolins there!—Thou wilt not, wilt thou?
Blow, and split thyself.

2 *Sailor.* But sea-room, an the brine and cloudy billow kiss the moon, I care not.

1 *Sailor.* Sir, your queen must overboard; the sea works high, the wind is loud, and will not lie till the ship be cleared of the dead.

Pericles. That 's your superstition.

1 *Sailor.* Pardon us, sir; with us at sea it hath been still observed, and we are strong in custom. Therefore briefly yield her; for she must overboard straight.

Pericles. As you think meet.—Most wretched queen!

Lychorida. Here she lies, sir.

Pericles. A terrible childbed hast thou had, my dear;
No light, no fire: the unfriendly elements
Forgot thee utterly; nor have I time
To give thee hallow'd to the grave, but straight
Must cast thee, scarcely coffin'd, in the ooze;
Where, for a monument upon thy bones,
And aye-remaining lamps, the belching whale
And humming water must o'erwhelm thy corpse,
Lying with simple shells.—O Lychorida,
Bid Nestor bring me spices, ink and paper,
My casket and my jewels; and bid Nicander
Bring me the satin coffer: lay the babe
Upon the pillow. Hie thee, whiles I say
A priestly farewell to her; suddenly, woman.
[*Exit Lychorida.*

2 *Sailor.* Sir, we have a chest beneath the hatches, caulked and bitumed ready.

Pericles. I thank thee. Mariner, say what coast is this?

2 *Sailor.* We are near Tarsus.

Pericles. Thither, gentle mariner,
Alter thy course for Tyre. When canst thou reach it?

2 *Sailor.* By break of day, if the wind cease.

Pericles. O, make for Tarsus!—
There will I visit Cleon, for the babe
Cannot hold out to Tyrus; there I 'll leave it
At careful nursing.—Go thy ways, good mariner;
I 'll bring the body presently. [*Exeunt.*

SCENE II. *Ephesus. A Room in Cerimon's House.*

Enter CERIMON, *with a* Servant, *and some shipwrecked Persons.*

Cerimon. Philemon, ho!

Enter PHILEMON.

Philemon. Doth my lord call?
Cerimon. Get fire and meat for these poor men;
'T has been a turbulent and stormy night.
Servant. I have been in many; but such a night as this,
Till now, I ne'er endur'd.
Cerimon. Your master will be dead ere you return;
There 's nothing can be minister'd to nature
That can recover him.—[*To Philemon*] Give this to the pothecary,
And tell me how it works. [*Exeunt all but Cerimon.*

Enter two Gentlemen.

1 *Gentleman.* Good morrow.
2 *Gentleman.* Good morrow to your lordship.
Cerimon. Gentlemen,
Why do you stir so early?
1 *Gentleman.* Sir,
Our lodgings, standing bleak upon the sea,
Shook as the earth did quake;
The very principals did seem to rend,
And all to topple: pure surprise and fear
Made me to quit the house.
2 *Gentleman.* That is the cause we trouble you so early;
'T is not our husbandry.
Cerimon. O, you say well.
1 *Gentleman.* But I much marvel that your lordship, having
Rich tire about you, should at these early hours

Shake off the golden slumber of repose.
'T is most strange,
Nature should be so conversant with pain,
Being thereto not compell'd.

Cerimon. I held it ever,
Virtue and cunning were endowments greater
Than nobleness and riches; careless heirs
May the two latter darken and expend,
But immortality attends the former,
Making a man a god. 'T is known, I ever
Have studied physic, through which secret art,
By turning o'er authorities, I have,
Together with my practice, made familiar
To me and to my aid the blest infusions
That dwell in vegetives, in metals, stones,
And I can speak of the disturbances
That nature works, and of her cures; which doth give me
A more content in course of true delight
Than to be thirsty after tottering honour,
Or tie my treasure up in silken bags,
To please the fool and death.

2 *Gentleman.* Your honour has through Ephesus pour'd forth
Your charity, and hundreds call themselves
Your creatures, who by you have been restor'd;
And not your knowledge, your personal pain, but even
Your purse, still open, hath built Lord Cerimon
Such strong renown as time shall never raze.

Enter two or three Servants *with a chest.*

1 *Servant.* So; lift there.

Cerimon. What is that?

1 *Servant.* Sir, even now
Did the sea toss upon our shore this chest;
'T is of some wrack.

Cerimon. Set 't down, let 's look upon 't.

2 *Gentleman.* 'T is like a coffin, sir.
Cerimon. Whate'er it be,
'T is wondrous heavy. Wrench it open straight;
If the sea's stomach be o'ercharg'd with gold,
'T is a good constraint of fortune it belches upon us.
2 *Gentleman.* 'T is so, my lord.
Cerimon. How close 't is caulk'd and bitum'd!
Did the sea cast it up?
1 *Servant.* I never saw so huge a billow, sir,
As toss'd it upon shore.
Cerimon. Wrench it open;
Soft! it smells most sweetly in my sense.
2 *Gentleman.* A delicate odour.
Cerimon. As ever hit my nostril. So up with it.—
O you most potent gods! what 's here? a corse!
1 *Gentleman.* Most strange!
Cerimon. Shrouded in cloth of state; balm'd and entreasur'd
With full bags of spices! A passport too!
Apollo, perfect me in the characters! [*Reads from a scroll.*
'*Here I give to understand,*
If e'er this coffin drive a-land,
I, King Pericles, have lost
This queen, worth all our mundane cost.
Who finds her, give her burying;
She was the daughter of a king.
Besides this treasure for a fee,
The gods requite his charity!'
If thou liv'st, Pericles, thou hast a heart
That even cracks for woe! This chanc'd to-night.
2 *Gentleman.* Most likely, sir.
Cerimon. Nay, certainly to-night;
For look how fresh she looks! They were too rough
That threw her in the sea.—Make a fire within:
Fetch hither all my boxes in my closet.— [*Exit a Servant.*

Death may usurp on nature many hours,
And yet the fire of life kindle again
The o'erpress'd spirits. I heard of an Egyptian
That had nine hours lien dead,
Who was by good appliance recovered.

Re-enter a Servant, *with boxes, napkins, and fire.*

Well said, well said; the fire and cloths.—
The rough and woeful music that we have,
Cause it to sound, beseech you.—
The vial once more.—How thou stirr'st, thou block! -
The music there!—I pray you, give her air.—
Gentlemen,
This queen will live: nature awakes; a warmth
Breathes out of her. She hath not been entranc'd
Above five hours; see how she gins to blow
Into life's flower again!

1 *Gentleman.* The heavens,
Through you, increase our wonder and set up
Your fame for ever.

Cerimon. She is alive; behold,
Her eyelids, cases to those heavenly jewels
Which Pericles hath lost,
Begin to part their fringes of bright gold;
The diamonds of a most praised water
Do appear, to make the world twice rich.—Live,
And make us weep to hear your fate, fair creature,
Rare as you seem to be. [*She moves.*

Thaisa. O dear Diana,
Where am I? Where 's my lord? What world is this?

2 *Gentleman.* Is not this strange?

1 *Gentleman.* Most rare.

Cerimon. Hush, my gentle neighbours!
Lend me your hands; to the next chamber bear her.
Get linen; now this matter must be look'd to,

For her relapse is mortal. Come, come;
And Æsculapius guide us! [*Exeunt, carrying her away.*

SCENE III. *Tarsus. A Room in Cleon's House.*

Enter PERICLES, CLEON, DIONYZA, *and* LYCHORIDA *with* MARINA *in her arms.*

Pericles. Most honour'd Cleon, I must needs be gone;
My twelve months are expir'd, and Tyrus stands
In a litigious peace. You, and your lady,
Take from my heart all thankfulness! The gods
Make up the rest upon you!

Cleon. Your shafts of fortune, though they hurt you mortally,
Yet glance full wanderingly on us.

Dionyza. O your sweet queen!
That the strict fates had pleas'd you had brought her hither,
To have bless'd mine eyes with her!

Pericles. We cannot but obey
The powers above us. Could I rage and roar
As doth the sea she lies in, yet the end
Must be as 't is. My gentle babe Marina—whom,
For she was born at sea, I have nam'd so—here
I charge your charity withal, leaving her
The infant of your care; beseeching you
To give her princely training, that she may be
Manner'd as she is born.

Cleon. Fear not, my lord, but think
Your grace, that fed my country with your corn,
For which the people's prayers still fall upon you,
Must in your child be thought on. If neglection
Should therein make me vile, the common body,
By you reliev'd, would force me to my duty;
But if to that my nature need a spur,

The gods revenge it upon me and mine,
To the end of generation!

Pericles. I believe you;
Your honour and your goodness teach me to 't,
Without your vow.—Till she be married, madam,
By bright Diana, whom we honour, all
Unscissar'd shall this hair of mine remain,
Though I show ill in 't. So I take my leave.
Good madam, make me blessed in your care
In bringing up my child.

Dionyza. I have one myself,
Who shall not be more dear to my respect
Than yours, my lord.

Pericles. Madam, my thanks and prayers.

Cleon. We 'll bring your grace e'en to the edge o' the shore,
Then give you up to the mask'd Neptune and
The gentlest winds of heaven.

Pericles. I will embrace
Your offer. Come, dear'st madam.—O, no tears,
Lychorida, no tears!
Look to your little mistress, on whose grace
You may depend hereafter.—Come, my lord. [*Exeunt.*

SCENE IV. *Ephesus. A Room in Cerimon's House.*

Enter CERIMON *and* THAISA.

Cerimon. Madam, this letter, and some certain jewels,
Lay with you in your coffer, which are now
At your command. Know you the character?

Thaisa. It is my lord's.
That I was shipp'd at sea, I well remember,
Even on my eaning time, but whether there
Deliver'd, by the holy gods,
I cannot rightly say. But since King Pericles,

My wedded lord, I ne'er shall see again,
A vestal livery will I take me to,
And never more have joy.
Cerimon. Madam, if this you purpose as you speak,
Diana's temple is not distant far,
Where you may abide till your date expire.
Moreover, if you please, a niece of mine
Shall there attend you.
Thaisa. My recompense is thanks, that 's all;
Yet my good will is great, though the gift small. [*Exeunt.*

ACT IV.

Enter GOWER.

Gower. Imagine Pericles arriv'd at Tyre,
Welcom'd and settled to his own desire.
His woeful queen we leave at Ephesus,
Unto Diana there a votaress.
Now to Marina bend your mind,
Whom our fast-growing scene must find
At Tarsus, and by Cleon train'd
In music, letters; who hath gain'd

Of education all the grace,
Which makes her both the heart and place
Of general wonder. But, alack,
That monster envy, oft the wrack
Of earned praise, Marina's life
Seeks to take off by treason's knife.
And in this kind hath our Cleon
One daughter, and a wench full grown,
Even ripe for marriage-rite: this maid
Hight Philoten; and it is said
For certain in our story, she
Would ever with Marina be:
But when she weav'd the sleided silk
With fingers long, small, white as milk,
Or when she would with sharp needle wound
The cambric, which she made more sound
By hurting it; or when to the lute
She sung, and made the night-bird mute,
That still records with moan; or when
She would with rich and constant pen
Vail to her mistress Dian; still
This Philoten contends in skill
With absolute Marina: so
With the dove of Paphos might the crow
Vie feathers white. Marina gets
All praises, which are paid as debts,
And not as given. This so darks
In Philoten all graceful marks,
That Cleon's wife, with envy rare,
A present murtherer does prepare
For good Marina, that her daughter
Might stand peerless by this slaughter.
The sooner her vile thoughts to stead,
Lychorida, our nurse, is dead;
And cursed Dionyza hath
The pregnant instrument of wrath
Prest for this blow. The unborn event
I do commend to your content:
Only I carry winged time
Post on the lame feet of my rhyme;
Which never could I so convey,
Unless your thoughts went on my way.

Dionyza does appear,
With Leonine, a murtherer. [*Exit.*

SCENE I. *Tarsus. An open Place near the Sea-shore.*

Enter DIONYZA *and* LEONINE.

Dionyza. Thy oath remember; thou hast sworn to do 't:
'T is but a blow, which never shall be known.
Thou canst not do a thing in the world so soon,
To yield thee so much profit. Let not conscience,
Which is but cold, inflaming love i' thy bosom,
Inflame too nicely; nor let pity, which
Even women have cast off, melt thee, but be
A soldier to thy purpose.

Leonine. I will do 't; but yet she is a goodly creature.

Dionyza. The fitter, then, the gods should have her. Here she comes weeping for her old nurse's death. Thou art resolved?

Leonine. I am resolved.

Enter MARINA, *with a basket of flowers.*

Marina. No, I will rob Tellus of her weed,
To strew thy green with flowers; the yellows, blues,
The purple violets, and marigolds,
Shall as a carpet hang upon thy grave,
While summer-days do last.—Ay me! poor maid,
Born in a tempest, when my mother died,
This world to me is like a lasting storm,
Whirring me from my friends.

Dionyza. How now, Marina? why do you keep alone?
How chance my daughter is not with you? Do not
Consume your blood with sorrowing; you have
A nurse of me. Lord, how your favour 's chang'd
With this unprofitable woe!
Come, give me your flowers, ere the sea mar them.

Walk with Leonine; the air is quick there,
And it pierces and sharpens the stomach.—Come,
Leonine, take her by the arm, walk with her.

Marina. No, I pray you;
I 'll not bereave you of your servant.

Dionyza. Come, come;
I love the king your father, and yourself,
With more than foreign heart. We every day
Expect him here; when he shall come and find
Our paragon to all reports thus blasted,
He will repent the breadth of his great voyage,
Blame both my lord and me, that we have taken
No care to your best courses. Go, I pray you,
Walk, and be cheerful once again; reserve
That excellent complexion, which did steal
The eyes of young and old. Care not for me;
I can go home alone.

Marina. Well, I will go;
But yet I have no desire to it.

Dionyza. Come, come, I know 't is good for you.—
Walk half an hour, Leonine, at the least.
Remember what I have said.

Leonine. I warrant you, madam.

Dionyza. I 'll leave you, my sweet lady, for a while.
Pray, walk softly, do not heat your blood;
What! I must have a care of you.

Marina. My thanks, sweet madam.—
[*Exit Dionyza.*
Is this wind westerly that blows?

Leonine. South-west.

Marina. When I was born, the wind was north.

Leonine. Was 't so?

Marina. My father, as nurse said, did never fear,
But cried 'Good seamen!' to the sailors, galling
His kingly hands, haling ropes,

And, clasping to the mast, endur'd a sea
That almost burst the deck.
Leonine. When was this?
Marina. When I was born.
Never was waves nor wind more violent;
And from the ladder-tackle washes off
A canvas-climber. 'Ha!' says one, 'wilt out?'
And with a dropping industry they skip
From stem to stern; the boatswain whistles, and
The master calls and trebles their confusion.
Leonine. Come, say your prayers.
Marina. What mean you?
Leonine. If you require a little space for prayer,
I grant it: pray; but be not tedious,
For the gods are quick of ear, and I am sworn
To do my work with haste.
Marina. Why will you kill me?
Leonine. To satisfy my lady.
Marina. Why would she have me kill'd?
Now, as I can remember, by my troth,
I never did her hurt in all my life;
I never spake bad word, nor did ill turn
To any living creature: believe me, la,
I never kill'd a mouse, nor hurt a fly.
I trod upon a worm against my will,
But I wept for it. How have I offended,
Wherein my death might yield her any profit,
Or my life imply her any danger?
Leonine. My commission
Is not to reason of the deed, but do it.
Marina. You will not do 't for all the world, I hope.
You are well favour'd, and your looks foreshow
You have a gentle heart. I saw you lately,
When you caught hurt in parting two that fought.
Good sooth, it show'd well in you; do so now:

Your lady seeks my life; come you between,
And save poor me, the weaker.

Leonine. I am sworn,
And will dispatch. [*He seizes her.*

Enter Pirates.

1 *Pirate.* Hold, villain! [*Leonine runs away.*

2 *Pirate.* A prize! a prize!

3 *Pirate.* Half-part, mates, half-part!
Come, let 's have her aboard suddenly.
[*Exeunt Pirates with Marina.*

Re-enter LEONINE.

Leonine. These roguing thieves serve the great pirate Valdes,
And they have seiz'd Marina. Let her go;
There 's no hope she will return. I 'll swear she 's dead,
And thrown into the sea.—But I 'll see further;
Perhaps they will but please themselves upon her,
Not carry her aboard. If she remain,
Whom they have ravish'd must by me be slain. [*Exit.*

SCENE II. *Mytilene. A Room in a Brothel.*

Enter PANDAR, Bawd, and BOULT.

Pandar. Boult!

Boult. Sir?

Pandar. Search the market narrowly; Mytilene is full of gallants. We lost too much money this mart by being too wenchless.

Boult. I 'll go search the market. [*Exit.*

Pandar. Three or four thousand chequins were as pretty a proportion to live quietly, and so give over.

Bawd. Why to give over, I pray you? is it a shame to get when we are old?

Pandar. O, our credit comes not in like the commodity, nor the commodity wages not with the danger: therefore, if in our youths we could pick up some pretty estate, 't were not amiss to keep our door hatched. Besides, the sore terms we stand upon with the gods will be strong with us for giving over.

Bawd. Come, other sorts offend as well as we.

Pandar. As well as we! ay, and better too; we offend worse. Neither is our profession any trade; it 's no calling. But here comes Boult.

Re-enter BOULT, *with the* Pirates *and* MARINA.

Bawd. [*To Marina*] Come your ways.—My masters, you say she 's a virgin?

1 *Pirate.* O, sir, we doubt it not.

Boult. Master, I have gone through for this piece, you see: if you like her, so; if not, I have lost my earnest.

Bawd. Boult, has she any qualities?

Boult. She has a good face, speaks well, and has excellent good clothes; there 's no further necessity of qualities can make her be refused.

Bawd. What 's her price, Boult?

Boult. I cannot be bated one doit of a thousand pieces.

Pandar. Well, follow me, my masters, you shall have your money presently.—Wife, take her in.

[*Exeunt Boult, Pandar, and Pirates.*

Marina. Alack that Leonine was so slack, so slow!
He should have struck, not spoke; or that these pirates,
Not enough barbarous, had not o'erboard thrown me
For to seek my mother!

Bawd. Why lament you, pretty one?

Marina. That I am pretty.

Bawd. Come, the gods have done their part in you.

Marina. I accuse them not.

Bawd. You are lit into my hands, where you are like to live.

Marina. The more my fault,
To scape his hands where I was like to die.

Bawd. Ay, and you shall live in pleasure.

Marina. No.

Bawd. Yes, indeed shall you; you shall fare well. What! do you stop your ears?

Marina. Are you a woman?

Bawd. What would you have me be, an I be not a woman?

Marina. An honest woman, or not a woman.

Bawd. Marry, whip thee, gosling; I think I shall have something to do with you. Come, you 're a young foolish sapling, and must be bowed as I would have you.

Marina. The gods defend me!

Bawd. Come your ways; follow me. [*Exeunt.*

SCENE III. *Tarsus. A Room in Cleon's House.*

Enter CLEON *and* DIONYZA.

Dionyza. Why, are you foolish? Can it be undone?
Cleon. O Dionyza, such a piece of slaughter
The sun and moon ne'er look'd upon!
Dionyza. I think
You 'll turn a child again.
Cleon. Were I chief lord of all this spacious world,
I 'd give it to undo the deed. O lady,
Much less in blood than virtue, yet a princess
To equal any single crown o' the earth
I' the justice of compare! O villain Leonine!
Whom thou hast poison'd too.
If thou hadst drunk to him, 't had been a kindness
Becoming well thy fact; what canst thou say
When noble Pericles shall demand his child?
Dionyza. That she is dead. Nurses are not the fates,
To foster it, nor ever to preserve.
She died at night; I 'll say so. Who can cross it?
Unless you play the pious innocent,
And for an honest attribute cry out
'She died by foul play.'
Cleon. O, go to. Well, well,
Of all the faults beneath the heavens, the gods
Do like this worst.
Dionyza. Be one of those that think

The petty wrens of Tarsus will fly hence,
And open this to Pericles. I do shame
To think of what a noble strain you are,
And of how coward a spirit.

Cleon. To such proceeding
Who ever but his approbation added,
Though not his prime consent, he did not flow
From honourable sources.

Dionyza. Be it so, then;
Yet none does know, but you, how she came dead,
Nor none can know, Leonine being gone.
She did distain my child, and stood between
Her and her fortunes; none would look on her,
But cast their gazes on Marina's face,
Whilst ours was blurted at and held a malkin
Not worth the time of day. It pierc'd me thorough;
And though you call my course unnatural,
You not your child well loving, yet I find
It greets me as an enterprise of kindness
Perform'd to your sole daughter.

Cleon. Heavens forgive it!

Dionyza. And as for Pericles,
What should he say? We wept after her hearse,
And yet we mourn; her monument
Is almost finish'd, and her epitaphs
In glittering golden characters express
A general praise to her, and care in us
At whose expense 't is done.

Cleon. Thou art like the harpy,
Which, to betray, dost, with thine angel's face,
Seize with thine eagle's talons.

Dionyza. You are like one that superstitiously
Doth swear to the gods that winter kills the flies;
But yet I know you 'll do as I advise. [*Exeunt*

Scene IV.

Enter Gower, *before the Monument of Marina at Tarsus.*

Gower. Thus time we waste, and longest leagues make short,
Sail seas in cockles, have an wish but for 't;
Making, to take your imagination,
From bourn to bourn, region to region.
By you being pardon'd, we commit no crime
To use one language in each several clime
Where our scenes seem to live. I do beseech you
To learn of me, who stand i' the gaps to teach you,
The stages of our story. Pericles
Is now again thwarting the wayward seas,
Attended on by many a lord and knight,
To see his daughter, all his life's delight.
Old Escanes, whom Helicanus late
Advanc'd in time to great and high estate,
Is left to govern. Bear you it in mind,
Old Helicanus goes along behind.
Well-sailing ships and bounteous winds have brought
This king to Tarsus,—think his pilot thought;
So with his steerage shall your thoughts grow on,—
To fetch his daughter home, who first is gone.
Like motes and shadows see them move awhile;
Your ears unto your eyes I 'll reconcile.

Dumb Show.

Enter Pericles, *at one door, with all his train;* Cleon *and* Dionyza, *at the other.* Cleon *shows* Pericles *the tomb; whereat* Pericles *makes lamentation, puts on sackcloth, and in a mighty passion departs. Then exeunt* Cleon *and* Dionyza.

See how belief may suffer by foul show!
This borrow'd passion stands for true old woe;
And Pericles, in sorrow all devour'd,
With sighs shot through and biggest tears o'ershower'd,
Leaves Tarsus and again embarks. He swears
Never to wash his face, nor cut his hairs;
He puts on sackcloth, and to sea. He bears
A tempest, which his mortal vessel tears,

And yet he rides it out. Now please you wit
The epitaph is for Marina writ
By wicked Dionyza.

[*Reads the inscription on Marina's monument.*

'*The fairest, sweet'st, and best lies here,*
Who wither'd in her spring of year.
She was of Tyrus the king's daughter,
On whom foul death hath made this slaughter.
Marina was she call'd; and at her birth,
Thetis, being proud, swallow'd some part o' the earth:
Therefore the earth, fearing to be o'erflow'd,
Hath Thetis' birth-child on the heavens bestow'd;
Wherefore she does, and swears she'll never stint,
Make raging battery upon shores of flint.'

No visor does become black villany
So well as soft and tender flattery.
Let Pericles believe his daughter 's dead,
And bear his courses to be ordered
By Lady Fortune; while our scene must play
His daughter's woe and heavy well-a-day
In her unholy service. Patience, then,
And think you now are all in Mytilene. [*Exit.*

SCENE V. *Mytilene. A Street before the Brothel.*

Enter, from the brothel, two Gentlemen.

1 *Gentleman.* Did you ever hear the like?

2 *Gentleman.* No, nor never shall do in such a place as this, she being once gone.

1 *Gentleman.* But to have divinity preached there! did you ever dream of such a thing?

2 *Gentleman.* No, no. Come, I am for no more bawdy-houses; shall 's go hear the vestals sing?

1 *Gentleman.* I 'll do any thing now that is virtuous. [*Exeunt.*

SCENE VI. *The Same. A Room in the Brothel.*

Enter Pandar, Bawd, *and* BOULT.

Pandar. Well, I had rather than twice the worth of her she had ne'er come here.

Bawd. Fie, fie upon her! she has me her quirks, her reasons, her master reasons, her prayers, her knees; that she would make a puritan of the devil, if he should cheapen a kiss of her.—Here comes the Lord Lysimachus disguised.

Boult. We should have both lord and lown, if the peevish baggage would but give way to customers.

Enter LYSIMACHUS.

Lysimachus. How now! How a dozen of virginities?

Bawd. Now, the gods to-bless your honour!

Boult. I am glad to see your honour in good health.

Lysimachus. You may so; 't is the better for you that your resorters stand upon sound legs. How now, wholesome iniquity! have you that a man may deal withal, and defy the surgeon?

Bawd. We have here one, sir, if she would—but there never came her like in Mytilene.

Lysimachus. Well, call forth, call forth. [*Exit Boult.*

Bawd. For flesh and blood, sir, white and red, you shall see a rose; and she were a rose indeed, if she had but—

Lysimachus. What, prithee?

Bawd. O, sir, I can be modest.—Here comes that which grows to the stalk; never plucked yet, I can assure you.

Re-enter BOULT *with* MARINA.

Is she not a fair creature?

Lysimachus. Faith, she would serve after a long voyage at sea. Well, there 's for you; leave us.

Bawd. I beseech your honour, give me leave; a word, and I 'll have done presently.

Lysimachus. I beseech you, do.

Bawd. [*To Marina*] First, I would have you note, this is an honourable man.

Marina. I desire to find him so, that I may worthily note him.

Bawd. Next, he 's the governor of this country, and a man whom I am bound to.

Marina. If he govern the country, you are bound to him indeed; but how honourable he is in that, I know not.

Bawd. Pray you, without any more virginal fencing, will you use him kindly? He will line your apron with gold.

Marina. What he will do graciously, I will thankfully receive.

Lysimachus. Ha' you done?

Bawd. Come, we will leave his honour and her together. Go thy ways. [*Exeunt Bawd, Pandar, and Boult.*

Marina. If you were born to honour, show it now;
If put upon you, make the judgment good
That thought you worthy of it.

Lysimachus. How 's this? how 's this? Some more; be sage.

Marina. For me,
That am a maid, though most ungentle fortune
Have plac'd me in this sty, O, that the gods
Would set me free from this unhallow'd place,
Though they did change me to the meanest bird
That flies i' the purer air!

Lysimachus. I did not think
Thou couldst have spoke so well, ne'er dream'd thou couldst.
Had I brought hither a corrupted mind,
Thy speech had alter'd it. Hold, here 's gold for thee.
Persever in that clear way thou goest,
And the gods strengthen thee!

Marina. The good gods preserve you!

Lysimachus. For me, be you thoughten
That I came with no ill intent; for to me
The very doors and windows savour vilely.
Fare thee well. Thou art a piece of virtue, and
I doubt not but thy training hath been noble.
Hold, here 's more gold for thee.
A curse upon him, die he like a thief,
That robs thee of thy goodness! If thou dost
Hear from me, it shall be for thy good.

Re-enter BOULT.

Boult. I beseech your honour, one piece for me.

Lysimachus. Avaunt, thou damned door-keeper!
Your house, but for this virgin that doth prop it,
Would sink and overwhelm you. Away! [*Exit.*

Boult. Come, mistress; come your ways with me.

Marina. Prithee, tell me one thing first.

Boult. Come now, your one thing.

Marina. What canst thou wish thine enemy to be?

Boult. Why, I could wish him to be my master, or rather, my mistress.

Marina. Neither of these are so bad as thou art,
Since they do better thee in their command.
Thou hold'st a place, for which the pained'st fiend
Of hell would not in reputation change.

Boult. What would you have me do? go to the wars, would you? where a man may serve seven years for the loss of a leg, and have not money enough in the end to buy him a wooden one?

Marina. Do any thing but this thou doest. Empty
Old receptacles, or common sewers, of filth;
Serve by indenture to the common hangman:
Any of these ways are yet better than this;
For what thou professest, a baboon, could he speak,
Would own a name too dear. O, that the gods
Would safely deliver me from this place!
Here, here 's gold for thee.
If that thy master would gain by me,
Proclaim that I can sing, weave, sew, and dance,
With other virtues, which I 'll keep from boast;
And I will undertake all these to teach.
I doubt not but this populous city will
Yield many scholars.

Boult. Well, I will see what I can do for thee; if I can place thee, I will.

Marina. But amongst honest women.

Boult. Faith, my acquaintance lies little amongst them. But since my master and mistress have bought you, there 's no going but by their consent; therefore I will make them acquainted with your purpose, and I doubt not but I shall find them tractable enough. Come, I 'll do for thee what I can; come your ways. [*Exeunt.*

ACT V.

Enter GOWER.

Gower. Marina thus the brothel scapes, and chances
Into an honest house, our story says.
She sings like one immortal, and she dances
As goddess-like to her admired lays;
Deep clerks she dumbs, and with her needle composes
Nature's own shape, of bud, bird, branch, or berry,
That even her art sisters the natural roses;
Her inkle, silk, twin with the rubied cherry:
That pupils lacks she none of noble race,

Who pour their bounty on her, and her gain
She gives the cursed bawd. Here we her place,
And to her father turn our thoughts again,
Where we left him, on the sea. We there him lost;
Whence, driven before the winds, he is arriv'd
Here where his daughter dwells; and on this coast
Suppose him now at anchor. The city striv'd
God Neptune's annual feast to keep; from whence
Lysimachus our Tyrian ship espies,
His banners sable, trimm'd with rich expense,
And to him in his barge with fervour hies.
In your supposing once more put your sight
Of heavy Pericles: think this his bark;
Where what is done in action, more, if might,
Shall be discover'd; please you, sit and hark. [*Exit.*

SCENE I. *On board Pericles' ship, off Mytilene. A close pavilion on deck, with a curtain before it; Pericles within it, reclining on a couch. A barge lying beside the Tyrian vessel.*

Enter two Sailors, *one belonging to the Tyrian vessel, the other to the barge; to them* HELICANUS.

Tyrian Sailor. [*To the Sailor of Mytilene*] Where is lord Helicanus? he can resolve you.
O, here he is.—
Sir, there 's a barge put off from Mytilene,
And in it is Lysimachus the governor,
Who craves to come aboard. What is your will?

Helicanus. That he have his. Call up some gentlemen.

Tyrian Sailor. Ho, gentlemen! my lord calls.

Enter two or three Gentlemen.

1 *Gentleman.* Doth your lordship call?

Helicanus. Gentlemen, there 's some of worth would come aboard;
I pray ye, greet them fairly.

[*The Gentlemen and the two Sailors descend, and go on board the barge.*

Enter, from thence, LYSIMACHUS *and* Lords; *with the* Gentlemen *and the two* Sailors.

Tyrian Sailor. Sir,
This is the man that can, in aught you would,
Resolve you.

Lysimachus. Hail, reverend sir! the gods preserve you!

Helicanus. And you, sir, to outlive the age I am,
And die as I would do.

Lysimachus. You wish me well.
Being on shore, honouring of Neptune's triumphs,
Seeing this goodly vessel ride before us,
I made to it, to know of whence you are.

Helicanus. First, what is your place?

Lysimachus. I am the governor of this place you lie before.

Helicanus. Sir,
Our vessel is of Tyre, in it the king;
A man who for this three months hath not spoken
To any one, nor taken sustenance
But to prorogue his grief.

Lysimachus. Upon what ground is his distemperature?

Helicanus. 'T would be too tedious to repeat;
But the main grief springs from the loss
Of a beloved daughter and a wife.

Lysimachus. May we not see him?

Helicanus. You may;
But bootless is your sight: he will not speak
To any.

Lysimachus. Yet let me obtain my wish.

Helicanus. Behold him. [*Pericles discovered.*] This was a goodly person,
Till the disaster that, one mortal night,
Drove him to this.

Lysimachus. Sir king, all hail! the gods preserve you!
Hail, royal sir!

Helicanus. It is in vain; he will not speak to you.
1 *Lord.* Sir,
We have a maid in Mytilene, I durst wager,
Would win some words of him.
Lysimachus. 'T is well bethought.
She, questionless, with her sweet harmony
And other chosen attractions, would allure,
And make a battery through his deafen'd parts,
Which now are midway stopp'd.
She is all happy as the fair'st of all,
And with her fellow maids is now upon
The leafy shelter that abuts against
The island's side.
[*Whispers a Lord, who goes off in the barge of Lysimachus.*
Helicanus. Sure, all 's effectless; yet nothing we 'll omit
That bears recovery's name. But, since your kindness
We have stretch'd thus far, let us beseech you
That for our gold we may provision have,
Wherein we are not destitute for want,
But weary for the staleness.
Lysimachus. O, sir, a courtesy
Which if we should deny, the most just gods
For every graff would send a caterpillar,
And so afflict our province. Yet once more
Let me entreat to know at large the cause
Of your king's sorrow.
Helicanus. Sit, sir, I will recount it to you.—
But, see, I am prevented.

Re-enter the Lord, *with* Marina *and a young* Lady.

Lysimachus. O, here is
The lady that I sent for.—Welcome, fair one!
Is 't not a goodly presence?
Helicanus. She 's a gallant lady.

Lysimachus. She 's such a one, that, were I well assur'd
Came of a gentle kind and noble stock,
I 'd wish no better choice, and think me rarely wed.—
Fair one, all goodness that consists in bounty
Expect even here, where is a kingly patient.
If that thy prosperous and artificial feat
Can draw him but to answer thee in aught,
Thy sacred physic shall receive such pay
As thy desires can wish.
Marina. Sir, I will use
My utmost skill in his recovery,
Provided
That none but I and my companion maid
Be suffer'd to come near him.
Lysimachus. Come, let us leave her;
And the gods make her prosperous! [*Marina sings.*
Lysimachus. Mark'd he your music?
Marina. No, nor look'd on us.
Lysimachus. See, she will speak to him.
Marina. Hail, sir! my lord, lend ear.
Pericles. Hum, ha!
Marina. I am a maid,
My lord, that ne'er before invited eyes,
But have been gaz'd on like a comet; she speaks,
My lord, that, may be, hath endur'd a grief
Might equal yours, if both were justly weigh'd.
Though wayward fortune did malign my state,
My derivation was from ancestors
Who stood equivalent with mighty kings;
But time hath rooted out my parentage,
And to the world and awkward casualties
Bound me in servitude. [*Aside*] I will desist;
But there is something glows upon my cheek,
And whispers in mine ear 'Go not till he speak.'
Pericles. My fortunes—parentage—good parentage—
To equal mine!—was it not thus? what say you?

Marina. I said, my lord, if you did know my parentage,
You would not do me violence.

Pericles. I do think so. Pray you, turn your eyes upon me.
You are like something that—What countrywoman?
Here of these shores?

Marina. No, nor of any shores;
Yet I was mortally brought forth, and am
No other than I appear.

Pericles. I am great with woe, and shall deliver weeping.
My dearest wife was like this maid, and such a one
My daughter might have been: my queen's square brows;
Her stature to an inch; as wand-like straight;
As silver-voic'd; her eyes as jewel-like
And cas'd as richly; in pace another Juno;
Who starves the ears she feeds, and makes them hungry,
The more she gives them speech.—Where do you live?

Marina. Where I am but a stranger; from the deck
You may discern the place.

Pericles. Where were you bred?
And how achiev'd you these endowments, which
You make more rich to owe?

Marina. If I should tell my history, it would seem
Like lies disdain'd in the reporting.

Pericles. Prithee, speak.
Falseness cannot come from thee; for thou look'st
Modest as Justice, and thou seem'st a palace
For the crown'd Truth to dwell in. I will believe thee,
And make my senses credit thy relation
To points that seem impossible; for thou look'st
Like one I lov'd indeed. What were thy friends?
Didst thou not say, when I did push thee back—
Which was when I perceiv'd thee—that thou cam'st
From good descending?

Marina. So indeed I did.

Pericles. Report thy parentage. I think thou said'st
Thou hadst been toss'd from wrong to injury,
And that thou thought'st thy griefs might equal mine,
If both were open'd.
Marina. Some such thing
I said, and said no more but what my thoughts
Did warrant me was likely.
Pericles. Tell thy story;
If thine consider'd prove the thousandth part
Of my endurance, thou art a man, and I
Have suffer'd like a girl: yet thou dost look
Like Patience gazing on kings' graves, and smiling
Extremity out of act. What were thy friends?
How lost thou them? Thy name, my most kind virgin?
Recount, I do beseech thee: come, sit by me.
Marina. My name is Marina.
Pericles. O, I am mock'd,
And thou by some incensed god sent hither
To make the world to laugh at me.
Marina. Patience, good sir,
Or here I'll cease.
Pericles. Nay, I'll be patient.
Thou little know'st how thou dost startle me,
To call thyself Marina.
Marina. The name
Was given me by one that had some power,
My father, and a king.
Pericles. How! a king's daughter?
And call'd Marina?
Marina. You said you would believe me;
But, not to be a troubler of your peace,
I will end here.
Pericles. But are you flesh and blood?
Have you a working pulse? and are no fairy?

No motion?—Well; speak on. Where were you born?
And wherefore call'd Marina?

Marina. Call'd Marina
For I was born at sea.

Pericles. At sea! what mother?

Marina. My mother was the daughter of a king,
Who died the minute I was born,
As my good nurse Lychorida hath oft
Deliver'd weeping.

Pericles. O, stop there a little!—
[*Aside*] This is the rarest dream that e'er dull sleep
Did mock sad fools withal: this cannot be;
My daughter 's buried.—Well; where were you bred?
I 'll hear you more, to the bottom of your story,
And never interrupt you.

Marina. You'll scarce believe me; 't were best I did give o'er.

Pericles. I will believe you by the syllable
Of what you shall deliver. Yet, give me leave:
How came you in these parts? where were you bred?

Marina. The king my father did in Tarsus leave me,
Till cruel Cleon, with his wicked wife,
Did seek to murther me, and having woo'd
A villain to attempt it, who having drawn to do 't,
A crew of pirates came and rescued me,
Brought me to Mytilene. But, good sir,
Whither will you have me? Why do you weep? It may be,
You think me an impostor: no, good faith;
I am the daughter to King Pericles,
If good King Pericles be.

Pericles. Ho, Helicanus!

Helicanus. Calls my lord?

Pericles. Thou art a grave and noble counsellor,
Most wise in general; tell me, if thou canst,
What this maid is, or what is like to be,
That thus hath made me weep?

Helicanus. I know not: but

Here is the regent, sir, of Mytilene
Speaks nobly of her.
Lysimachus. She would never tell
Her parentage; being demanded that,
She would sit still and weep.
Pericles. O Helicanus, strike me, honour'd sir;
Give me a gash, put me to present pain,
Lest this great sea of joys rushing upon me
O'erbear the shores of my mortality,
And drown me with their sweetness.—O, come hither,
Thou that beget'st him that did thee beget,
Thou that wast born at sea, buried at Tarsus,
And found at sea again!—O Helicanus,
Down on thy knees, thank the holy gods as loud
As thunder threatens us; this is Marina.—
What was thy mother's name? tell me but that,
For truth can never be confirm'd enough,
Though doubts did ever sleep.
Marina. First, sir, I pray,
What is your title?
Pericles. I am Pericles of Tyre; but tell me now
My drown'd queen's name, as in the rest you said
Thou hast been godlike perfect, and thou art
The heir of kingdoms and another life
To Pericles thy father.
Marina. Is it no more to be your daughter than
To say my mother's name was Thaisa?
Thaisa was my mother, who did end
The minute I began.
Pericles. Now, blessing on thee! rise; thou art my child.—
Give me fresh garments.—Mine own, Helicanus;
She is not dead at Tarsus, as she should have been,
By savage Cleon: she shall tell thee all;
When thou shalt kneel, and justify in knowledge
She is thy very princess.—Who is this?

Helicanus. Sir, 't is the governor of Mytilene,
Who, hearing of your melancholy state,
Did come to see you.

Pericles. I embrace you.—
Give me my robes.—I am wild in my beholding.—.
O heavens bless my girl!—But, hark, what music?—
Tell Helicanus, my Marina, tell him
O'er, point by point, for yet he seems to doubt,
How sure you are my daughter.—But, what music?

Helicanus. My lord, I hear none.

Pericles. None!
The music of the spheres!—List, my Marina.

Lysimachus. It is not good to cross him; give him way.

Pericles. Rarest sounds! Do ye not hear?

Lysimachus. Music, my lord? I hear—

Pericles. Most heavenly music!
It nips me unto listening, and thick slumber
Hangs upon mine eyes; let me rest. [*Sleeps.*

Lysimachus. A pillow for his head.—
So, leave him all.—Well, my companion friends,
If this but answer to my just belief,
I 'll well remember you. [*Exeunt all but Pericles.*

DIANA *appears to* PERICLES *as in a vision.*

Diana. My temple stands in Ephesus; hie thee thither,
And do upon mine altar sacrifice.
There, when my maiden priests are met together,
Before the people all,
Reveal how thou at sea didst lose thy wife;
To mourn thy crosses, with thy daughter's, call
And give them repetition to the life.
Or perform my bidding, or thou liv'st in woe;
Do it, and happy, by my silver bow!
Awake, and tell thy dream. [*Disappears.*

Pericles. Celestial Dian, goddess argentine,
I will obey thee.—Helicanus!

Re-enter HELICANUS, LYSIMACHUS, *and* MARINA.

Helicanus. Sir?
Pericles. My purpose was for Tarsus, there to strike
The inhospitable Cleon; but I am
For other service first: toward Ephesus
Turn our blown sails; eftsoons I 'll tell thee why.—
[*To Lysimachus*] Shall we refresh us, sir, upon your shore,
And give you gold for such provision
As our intents will need?
Lysimachus. Sir,
With all my heart; and, when you come ashore,
I have another suit.
Pericles. You shall prevail,
Were it to woo my daughter; for it seems
You have been noble towards her.
Lysimachus. Sir, lend me your arm.
Pericles. Come, my Marina. [*Exeunt.*

SCENE II.—*Enter* GOWER, *before the Temple of Diana at Ephesus.*

Gower. Now our sands are almost run;
More a little, and then dumb.
This, my last boon, give me,
For such kindness must relieve me,
That you aptly will suppose
What pageantry, what feats, what shows,
What minstrelsy, and pretty din,
The regent made in Mytilene
To greet the king. So he thriv'd
That he is promis'd to be wiv'd
To fair Marina; but in no wise
Till he had done his sacrifice,
As Dian bade: whereto being bound,
The interim, pray you, all confound.

In feather'd briefness sails are fill'd,
And wishes fall out as they 're will'd.
At Ephesus, the temple see,
Our king, and all his company.
That he can hither come so soon,
Is by your fancies' thankful doom. [*Exit.*

SCENE III.—*The Temple of Diana at Ephesus;* THAISA *standing near the Altar, as High-Priestess; a number of Virgins on each side;* CERIMON *and other Inhabitants of Ephesus attending.*

Enter PERICLES, *with his train;* LYSIMACHUS, HELICANUS, MARINA, *and a* Lady.

Pericles. Hail, Dian! to perform thy just command,
I here confess myself the king of Tyre,
Who, frighted from my country, did wed
At Pentapolis the fair Thaisa.
At sea in childbed died she, but brought forth
A maid-child call'd Marina, who, O goddess,
Wears yet thy silver livery. She at Tarsus
Was nurs'd with Cleon; who at fourteen years
He sought to murther, but her better stars
Brought her to Mytilene, 'gainst whose shore
Riding, her fortunes brought the maid aboard us,
Where, by her own most clear remembrance, she
Made known herself my daughter.

Thaisa. Voice and favour!
You are, you are—O royal Pericles! [*Faints.*

Pericles. What means the nun? she dies!—help, gentlemen!

Cerimon. Noble sir,
If you have told Diana's altar true,
This is your wife.

Pericles. Reverend appearer, no;
I threw her overboard with these very arms.

Cerimon. Upon this coast, I warrant you.
Pericles. 'T is most certain.
Cerimon. Look to the lady.—O, she 's but o'erjoy'd.
Early in blustering morn this lady was
Thrown upon this shore. I op'd the coffin,
Found there rich jewels, recover'd her, and plac'd her
Here in Diana's temple.
Pericles. May we see them?
Cerimon. Great sir, they shall be brought you to my house,
Whither I invite you. Look, Thaisa is
Recovered.
Thaisa. O, let me look!
If he be none of mine, my sanctity
Will to my sense bend no licentious ear,
But curb it, spite of seeing.—O, my lord,
Are you not Pericles? Like him you spake,
Like him you are; did you not name a tempest,
A birth, and death?
Pericles. The voice of dead Thaisa!
Thaisa. That Thaisa am I, supposed dead
And drown'd.
Pericles. Immortal Dian!
Thaisa. Now I know you better.
When we with tears parted Pentapolis,
The king my father gave you such a ring. [*Shows a ring.*
Pericles. This, this!—no more, you gods! your present kindness
Makes my past miseries sports; you shall do well,
That on the touching of her lips I may
Melt and no more be seen.—O, come, be buried
A second time within these arms.
Marina. My heart
Leaps to be gone into my mother's bosom. [*Kneels to Thaisa.*
Pericles. Look, who kneels here! Flesh of thy flesh, Thaisa;

Thy burden at the sea, and call'd Marina
For she was yielded there.

Thaisa. Blest, and mine own!

Helicanus. Hail, madam, and my queen!

Thaisa. I know you not.

Pericles. You have heard me say, when I did fly from Tyre,
I left behind an ancient substitute;
Can you remember what I call'd the man?
I have nam'd him oft.

Thaisa. 'T was Helicanus then.

Pericles. Still confirmation!
Embrace him, dear Thaisa; this is he.
Now do I long to hear how you were found,
How possibly preserv'd, and who to thank,
Besides the gods, for this great miracle.

Thaisa. Lord Cerimon, my lord; this man,
Through whom the gods have shown their power, that can
From first to last resolve you.

Pericles. Reverend sir,
The gods can have no mortal officer
More like a god than you. Will you deliver
How this dead queen re-lives?

Cerimon. I will, my lord.
Beseech you, first go with me to my house,
Where shall be shown you all was found with her:
How she came plac'd here in the temple,
No needful thing omitted.

Pericles. Pure Dian, bless thee for thy vision! I
Will offer night-oblations to thee.—Thaisa,
This prince, the fair-betrothed of your daughter,
Shall marry her at Pentapolis.—And now,
This ornament
Makes me look dismal will I clip to form;
And what this fourteen years no razor touch'd,
To grace thy marriage-day, I 'll beautify.

Thaisa. Lord Cerimon hath letters of good credit, sir,
My father 's dead.

Pericles. Heavens make a star of him!—Yet there, my queen,
We 'll celebrate their nuptials, and ourselves
Will in that kingdom spend our following days;
Our son and daughter shall in Tyrus reign.—
Lord Cerimon, we do our longing stay
To hear the rest untold.—Sir, lead 's the way. [*Exeunt.*

Enter GOWER.

Gower. In Antiochus and his daughter you have heard
Of monstrous lust the due and just reward;
In Pericles, his queen and daughter, seen,
Although assail'd with fortune fierce and keen,
Virtue preserv'd from fell destruction's blast,
Led on by heaven, and crown'd with joy at last;
In Helicanus may you well descry
A figure of truth, of faith, of loyalty;
In reverend Cerimon there well appears
The worth that learned charity aye wears;
For wicked Cleon and his wife, when fame
Had spread their cursed deed, the honour'd name
Of Pericles, to rage the city turn,
That him and his they in his palace burn;
The gods for murther seemed so content
To punish them, although not done, but meant.
So, on your patience evermore attending,
New joy wait on you! Here our play has ending. [*Exit*

NOTES.

ABBREVIATIONS USED IN THE NOTES.

Abbott (or Gr.), Abbott's *Shakespearian Grammar* (third edition).
A. S., Anglo-Saxon.
A. V., Authorized Version of the Bible (1611).
B. and F., Beaumont and Fletcher.
B. J., Ben Jonson.
Camb. ed., "Cambridge edition" of Shakespeare, edited by Clark and Wright.
Cf. (*confer*), compare.
Clarke, "Cassell's Illustrated Shakespeare," edited by Charles and Mary Cowden Clarke (London, n. d.).
Coll., Collier (second edition).
Coll. MS., Manuscript Corrections of Second Folio, edited by Collier.
D., Dyce (second edition).
H., Hudson ("Harvard" edition).
Halliwell, J. O. Halliwell (folio ed. of Shakespeare).
Id. (*idem*), the same.
K., Knight (second edition).
Nares, *Glossary*, edited by Halliwell and Wright (London, 1859).
Prol., Prologue.
S., Shakespeare.
Schmidt, A. Schmidt's *Shakespeare-Lexicon* (Berlin, 1874).
Sr., Singer.
St., Staunton.
Theo., Theobald.
V., Verplanck.
W., R. Grant White.
Walker, Wm. Sidney Walker's *Critical Examination of the Text of Shakespeare* (London, 1860).
Warb., Warburton.
Wb., Webster's Dictionary (revised quarto edition of 1879)
Worc., Worcester's Dictionary (quarto edition).

The abbreviations of the names of Shakespeare's Plays will be readily understood; as *T. N.* for *Twelfth Night*, *Cor.* for *Coriolanus*, 3 *Hen. VI.* for *The Third Part of King Henry the Sixth*, etc. *P. P.* refers to *The Passionate Pilgrim*; *V. and A.* to *Venus and Adonis*; *L. C.* to *Lover's Complaint*; and *Sonn.* to the *Sonnets*.

When the abbreviation of the name of a play is followed by a reference to *page*, Rolfe's edition of the play is meant.

The numbers of the lines (except for the present play) are those of the "Globe" ed.

NOTES.

GOWER'S MONUMENT.*

INTRODUCTION.

ILLUSTRATIVE PASSAGES FROM GOWER.—Knight gives the following extracts from Gower's *Confessio Amantis* (quoted here by permission) to illustrate the use made of the poem in the play:

* In St. Saviour's, Southwark, London. Gower had contributed largely to the restoration of the church, in which, in 1399, he had been married to Alice Groundolf by William of Wykeham, Bishop of Winchester. Stow describes the monument thus: "He lieth

ACT I.—"The father, when he understood
That they his daughter thus besought,
With all his wit he cast and sought
How that he might find a let;
And thus a statute then he set,
And in this wise his law he taxeth—
That what man that his daughter axeth,
But if he couth[1] his question
Assoil,[2] upon suggestion
Of certain things that befell,
The which he would unto him tell,
He should in certain lose his head.
And thus there were many dead,
Their heads standing on the gate,
Till at last, long and late,
For lack of answer in the wise,[3]
The remnant, that weren wise,
Eschewden to make essay.

* * * * *

The king declareth him the case
With stern look and sturdy cheer,
To him and said in this manner:
With felony I am up bore,
I eat, and have it nought forbore,
My mother's flesh, whose husband
My father for to seek I fonde,[4]
Which is the son of my wife.
Hereof I am inquisitive,
And who that can my tale save,
All quite[5] he shall my daughter have
Of his answer; and if he fail
He shall be dead without fail.
For thee, my son, quoth the king,
Be well advised of this thing
Which hath thy life in jeopardy.

* * * * *

This young prince forth he went,
And understood well what he meant,
Within his heart, as he was lered;[6]
That for to make him affered[7]

---

under a tomb of stone, with his image also of stone over him: the hair of his head auburn, long to his shoulders but curling up, and a small forked beard; on his head a chaplet like a coronet of four roses; a habit of purple, damasked down to his feet; a collar of esses gold about his neck; under his head the likeness of three books which he compiled."

[1] *Couth*—was able.
[2] *Assoil*—answer.
[3] *In the wise*—in the manner.
[4] *Fonde*—try.
[5] *Quite*—free.
[6] *Lered*—taught.
[7] *Affered*—afraid.

The king his time hath so delayed.
Whereof he dradde,[1] and was amayed[2]
Of treason that he die should,
For he the king his soth[3] told;
And suddenly the night's tide,
That more would he not abide,
All privily his barge he hent,[4]
And home again to Tyre he went.
And in his own wit he said,
For dread if he the king bewray'd,[5]
He knew so well the king's heart,
That death ne should he not asterte,[6]
The king would him so pursue.
But he that would his death eschew,
And knew all this to fore the hand
Forsake he thought his own land,
That there would he not abide;
For well he knew that on some side
This tyrant, of his felony,
By some manner of treachery
To grieve his body would not leave.

* * * * *

Antiochus, the great sire,
Which full of rancour and of ire
His heart beareth so, as ye heard,
Of that this prince of Tyre answer'd.
He had a fellow-bachelor,
Which was the privy councillor,
And Taliart by name he hight;
The king a strong poison dight
Within a box, and gold thereto,
In all haste, and bade him go
Straight unto Tyre, and for no cost
Ne spare, till he had lost
The prince, which he would spill.
And when the king hath said his will,
This Taliart in a galley
With all haste he took his way.
The wind was good, and saileth blive,[7]
Till he took land upon the rive[8]
Of Tyre, and forth with all anon
Into the burgh he gan to gon,
And took his inn, and bode a throw;[9]
But for he would not be know,

1 *Dradde*—dreaded.
2 *Amayed*—dismayed.
3 *Soth*—truth.
4 *Hent*—took to.
5 *Bewray'd*—discovered.
6 *Asterte*—escape.
7 *Blive*—quick.
8 *Rive*—coast.
9 *Throw*—time.

Disguised then he goeth him out,
He saw the weeping all about,
And axeth what the cause was.
And they him tolden all the case,
How suddenly the prince is go.
And when he saw that it was so,
And that his labour was in vain,
Anon he turneth home again:
And to the king when he came nigh,
He told of that he heard and sihe,[1]
How that the prince of Tyre is fled,
So was he come again unsped.
The king was sorry for a while,
But when he saw, that with no wile
He might achieve his cruelty,
He stint his wrath, and let him be.

* * * * *

But over this now for to tell
Of adventures, that befell
Unto this prince of whom ytold:
He hath his right course forth hold
By stern and needle,[2] till he came
To Tharse, and there his land he name.
A burgess rich of gold and fee
Was thilke time in that city,
Which cleped was Stranguilio,
His wife was Dionise also.
This young prince, as saith the book,
With him his herbergage[3] took;
And it befell that city so,
By fore time and then also,
Thurh[4] strong famine, which them lad,[5]
Was none that any wheat had.
Appollinus, when that he heard
The mischief how the city ferde,[6]
All freely of his own gift,
His wheat among them for to shift,
The which by ship he had brought,
He gave, and took of them right nought.
But sithen first the world began
Was never yet to such a man
More joy made, than they him made;
For they were all of him so glad,
That they for ever in remembrance
Made a figure in resemblance

---

[1] *Sihe*—saw.
[2] *Stern and needle*—stars and compass.
[3] *Herbergage*—lodging.
[4] *Thurh*—through.
[5] *Lad*—led, affected.
[6] *Ferde*—terrified.

Of him, and in common place
They set it up; so that his face
Might every manner man behold,
So that the city was behold.
It was of laton[1] over-gilt;
Thus hath he not his gift spilt."

ACT II.—" When him thought all grace away,
There came a fisher in the way,
And saw a man there naked stond,
And when that he hath understond
The cause, he hath of him great ruth,[2]
And only of his poor truth,
Of such clothes as he had
With great pity this lord he clad,
And he him thanketh, as he should,
And saith him that it shall be gold,
If ever he get his state again;
And pray'd that he would him seyn[3]
If nigh were any town for him.
He said, Yea, Pentapolim,
Where both king and queen dwellen.
When he this tale heard tellen
He gladdeth him, and gan beseech
That he the way him would teach;
And he him taught, and forth he went,
And prayed God with good intent
To send him joy after his sorrow.
It was not yet passed mid-morrow.

* * * * *

Then thitherward his way he name,[4]
Where soon upon the noon he came.
He eat such as he might get,
And forth anon, when he had eat,
He goeth to see the town about;
And came there as he found a rout
Of young lusty men withal;
And as it should then befall,
That day was set of such assise,
That they should in the land's guise,
As he heard of the people say,
The common game then play:
And cried was, that they should come
Unto the game, all and some

---

[1] *Laton*—mixed metal.
[2] *Ruth*—pity.
[3] *Seyn*—say.
[4] *Name*—takes.

Of them that ben[1] deliver[2] and wight,[3]
To do such mastery as they might.

* * * * *

And fell among them into game,
And there he won him such a name
So as the king himself accounteth
That he all other men surmounteth,
And bare the prize above them all.
The king bade that into his hall,
At supper-time, he shall be brought;
And he came there, and left it nought
Without company alone.
Was none so seemly of person,
Of visage, and of limbs both,
If that he had what to clothe.
At supper-time, nathless,
The king amid all the press
Let clap him up among them all,
And bade his marshal of his hall
To setten him in such degree
That he upon him might see.
The king was soon set and serv'd,
And he which hath his prize deserv'd,
After the king's own word,
Was made begin a middle board,
That both king and queen him sihe.[4]
He sat, and cast about his eye,
And saw the lords in estate,
And with himself wax in debate,
Thinking what he had lore;[5]
And such a sorrow he took therefore,
That he sat ever still, and thought.
As he which of no meat rought.[6]

* * * * *

The king beheld his heaviness,
And of his great gentleness
His daughter, which was fair and good,
And at the board before him stood,
As it was thilke[7] time usage,
He bade to go on his message,
And fonde[8] for to make him glad,
And she did as her father bade,
And goeth to him the soft pace,

---

[1] *Ben*—are.
[2] *Deliver*—nimble.
[3] *Wight*—active.
[4] *Sihe*—saw.
[5] *Lore*—lost.
[6] *Rought*—cared.
[7] *Thilke*—that same.
[8] *Fonde*—try.

And axeth whence and what he was,
And prayeth he should his thoughts leave.

* * * * *

When he hath harped all his fill
The king's hest to fulfil,
Away goeth dish, away goeth cup,
Down goeth the board, the cloth was up,
They risen, and gone out of hall.
The king his chamberlain let call,
And bade that he by all way
A chamber for this man purvey,
Which nigh his own chamber be.
It shall be do, my lord, quoth he.

* * * * *

"And when that he to chamber is come,
He hath into his council nome[1]
This man of Tyre, and let him see
This letter, and all the privity
The which his daughter to him sent.
And he his knee to ground bent
And thanketh him and her also;
And ere they went then a two,[2]
With good heart, and with good courage,
Of full love and full marriage
The king and he ben whole accorded.
And after, when it was recorded
Unto the daughter how it stood,
The gift of all the world's good
Ne should have made her half so blithe."

ACT III.—"They axen when the ship is come:
From Tyre, anon answered some.
And over this they saiden more,
The cause why they come for
Was for to seek, and for to find,
Appollinus, which is of kind
Their liege lord; and he appeareth,
And of the tale which he heareth
He was right glad; for they him told
That for vengeance, as God it would,
Antiochus, as men may wete,[3]
With thunder and lightning is sore smete.[4]
His daughter hath the same chance,
So be they both in o[5] balance.

* * * * *

---

[1] *Nome*—taken.
[2] *A two*—apart.
[3] *Wete*—know.
[4] *Smete*—smitten.
[5] *O*—one.

Lychorida for her office
Was take, which was a nourrice,
To wend with this young wife,
To whom was shape a woeful life.
Within a time, as it betid,
When they were in the sea amid,
Out of the north they saw a cloud:
The storm arose, the winds loud
They blewen many a dreadful blast,
The welkin was all overcast.
The dark night the sun hath under,
There was a great tempest of thunder.
The moon, and eke the stars both,
In black clouds they them clothe,
Whereof their bright look they hid.
This young lady wept and cried,
To whom no comfort might avail.
Of child she began travail,
Where she lay in a cabin close.
Her woeful lord from her arose,
And that was long ere any morrow,
So that in anguish and in sorrow
She was deliver'd all by night,
And dead in every man's sight.
But nathless for all this woe
A maid child was bore tho.[1]

* * * * *

The master shipman came and pray'd,
With other such as be therein,
And said that he may nothing win
Again the death, but they him rede,[2]
He be well ware, and take heed.
The sea by way of his nature
Receive may no creature,
Within himself as for to hold
The which is dead; for this they would,
As they councillen all about,
The dead body casten out:
For better it is, they saiden all,
That it of her so befal,
Than if they shoulden all spill.

* * * * *

I am, quoth he, but one alone;
So would I not for my person
There fell such adversity,
But when it may no better be,

---

[1] *Tho*—then. [2] *Rede*—advise.

Do then thus upon my word:
Let make a coffer strong of board,
That it be firm with lead and pitch.
Anon was made a coffer such
All ready brought unto his hand;
And when he saw, and ready found
This coffer made, and well enclowed,
The dead body was besowed
In cloth of gold, and laid therein.

* * * * *

I, king of Tyre, Appollinus,
Do all manner men to wit,
That hear and see this letter writ,
That, helpless without rede,[1]
Here lieth a king's daughter dead;
And who that happeth her to find,
For charity take in his mind,
And do so that she be begrave,[2]
With this treasure which he shall have.

* * * * *

Right as the corpse was thrown on land,
There came walking upon the strand
A worthy clerk, a surgeon,
And eke a great physician,
Of all that land the wisest one,
Which hight master Cerymon:
There were of his disciples some.
This master to the coffer is come,
And peyseth [3] there was somewhat in,
And bade them bear it to his inn,
And goeth himself forth withal.
All that shall fall, fall shall.

* * * * *

They laid her on a couch soft,
And with a sheet warmed oft.
Her cold breast began to heat,
Her heart also to flack [4] and beat.
This master hath her every joint
With certain oil and balm anoint,
And put a liquor in her mouth,
Which is to few clerks couth,[5]
So that she 'covereth at the last.
And first her eyen up she cast;

---

1 *Rede*—counsel; perhaps here medical aid.
2 *Begrave*—buried.
3 *Peyseth*—considereth.
4 *Flack*—flutter.
5 *Couth*—known.

And when she more of strength caught,
Her arms both forth she straught,[1]
Held up her hand, and piteously
She spake, and said, Ah! where am I?
Where is my lord? What world is this?
As she that wot nought how it is.

* * * * *

My daughter Thayse, by your leave,
I think shall with you bileave[2]
As for a time; and thus I pray
That she be kept by all way:
And when she hath of age more,
That she be set to books' lore.
And this avow to God I make,
That I shall never for her sake
My beard for no liking shave,
Till it befall that I have,
In convenable time of age,
Beset her unto marriage."

ACT IV.—"And for to speak how that it stood
Of Thayse his daughter, where she dwelleth
In Tharse, as the chronique telleth.
She was well kept, she was well looked,
She was well taught, she was well booked;
So well she sped in her youth
That she of every wisdom couth,
That for to seek in every lond
So wise another no man found,
Ne so well taught at man's eye;
But woe-worth, ever falls envy.

* * * * *

The treason and the time is shape,
So fell it that this churlish knape
Hath led this maiden where he would
Upon the strand, and what she should
She was a drad; and he out braid[3]
A rusty sword, and to her said,
Thou shalt be dead: alas, quoth she,
Why shall I so? So thus, quoth he,
My lady Dionise hath bade
Thou shalt be murder'd in this stede.
This maid then for fear shrihte,[4]
And for the love of God all-might

---

[1] *Straught*—stretched.
[2] *Bileave*—leave behind.
[3] *Braid*—started, drew.
[4] *Shrihte*—shrieked.

She pray'th, that for a little stound[1]
She might kneel upon the ground
Toward the heaven, for to crave
Her woeful soul that she may save.
And with this noise and with this cry
Out of a barge fast by,
Which hid was there on scomerfare,
Men start out, and weren ware
Of this felon: and he to go,
And she began to cry tho,[2]
Ha, mercy, help, for God's sake!
Into the barge they her take,
As thieves should, and forth they went.

* * * * *

If so be that thy master would
That I his gold increase should,
It may not fall by this way;
But suffer me to go my way
Out of this house, where I am in,
And I shall make him for to win
In some place else of the town,
Be so it be of religion,
Where that honest women dwell.
And thus thou might thy master tell,
That when I have a chamber there,
Let him do cry ay wide-where,[3]
What lord that hath his daughter dear,
And is in will that she shall lere[4]
Of such a school as is true,
I shall her teach of things new,
Which that none other woman can
In all this land.

* * * * *

Her epitaph of good assise[5]
Was writ about, and in this wise
It spake: O ye that this behold,
Lo, here lieth she, the which was hold
The fairest, and the flower of all,
Whose name Taysis men call.
The king of Tyre, Appollinus,
Her father was: now lieth she thus.
Fourteen year she was of age
When death her took to his viage."[6]

---

1 *Stound*—moment.
2 *Tho*—then.
3 *Wide-where*—far and near.
4 *Lere*—learn.
5 *Assise*—situation.
6 *Viage*—journey.

Act V.—"A messenger for her is gone,
And she came with her harp on hond;
And she said them, that she would fonde[1]
By all the ways that she can
To glad with this sorry man.
But what he was she wist nought,
But all the ship her hath besought,
That she her wits on him despend,[2]
In aunter[3] if he might amend,
And say it shall be well acquit.
When she hath understonden it
She goeth her down, there as he lay,
Where that she harpeth many a lay,
And like an angel sang withal.
But he no more than the wall
Took heed of anything he heard.
And when she saw that he so ferde[4]
She falleth with him into words,
And telleth him of sundry bordes,[5]
And asketh him demands strange,
Whereof she made his heart change;
And to her speech his ear he laid,
And hath marvel of that she said.
For in proverb and in problem
She spake, and bade he should deme[6]
In many a subtile question;
But he for no suggestion
Which toward him she could stere,[7]
He would not o[8] word answer,
But as a madman at the last,
His head weeping away he cast,
And half in wrath he bade her go:
But yet she would nought do so;
And in the dark forth she goeth
Till she him toucheth, and he wrothe,[9]
And after her with his hand
He smote: and thus when she him found
Diseased, courteously she said,—
Avoy,[10] my lord, I am a maid;
And if ye wist what I am,
And out of what lineage I came,
Ye would not be so salvage.
With that he sober'th his courage,

---

1 *Fonde*—try.
2 *Despend*—would expend.
3 *Aunter*—adventure.
4 *Ferde*—fared.
5 *Bordes*—countries.
6 *Deme*—judge.
7 *Stere*—stir.
8 *O*—one.
9 *Wrothe*—was angry.
10 *Avoy*—avoid.

And put away his heavy cheer;
But of them two a man may lere
What is to be so sibbe[1] of blood
None wist of other how it stood,
And yet the father at last
His heart upon this maid cast,
That he her loveth kindly;
And yet he wist never why,
But all was known ere that they went:
For God, which wot their whole intent,
Their hearts both he discloseth.
This king unto this maid opposeth,
And asketh first, what is her name,
And where she learned all this game,
And of what kin that she was come;
And she, that hath his words nome,[2]
Answereth, and saith, My name is Thaise,
That was some time well at ease.
In Tharse I was forth draw and fed,
There learned I till I was sped,
Of that I can: my father eke,
I not where that I should him seek:
He was a king men told me.
My mother drown'd was in the sea.
From point to point all she him told
That she hath long in heart hold,
And never durst make her moan
But only to this lord alone,
To whom her heart cannot hele,[3]
Turn it to woe, turn it to weal,
Turn it to good, turn it to harm.
And he then took her in his arm;
But such a joy as he then made
Was never seen: thus be they glad
That sorry hadden be to forn.[4]
From this day forth fortune hath sworn
To set them upward on the wheel:
So goeth the world, now woe, now weal.

* * * * *

With worthy knights environed,
The king himself hath abandoned
Into the temple in good intent.
The door is up, and in he went,
Where as, with great devotion
Of holy contemplation

---

[1] *Sibbe*—related.
[2] *Nome*—taken.
[3] *Hele*—hide.
[4] *To forn*—before.

Within his heart, he made his shrift,
And after that a rich gift
He off'reth with great reverence;
And there in open audience
Of them that stooden all about
He told them, and declareth out
His hap, such as him is befall:
There was no thing forget of all.
His wife, as it was God's grace,
Which was professed in the place
As she that was abbess there,
Unto his tale hath laid her ear.
She knew the voice, and the visage:
For pure joy, as in a rage,
She stretch'd unto him all at once,
And fell a swoon upon the stones
Whereof the temple-floor was paved.
She was anon with water laved,
Till she came to herself again,
And then she began to seyn,
Ah, blessed be the high soonde,[1]
That I may see mine husband,
Which whilom he and I were one.

* * * * *

Attaint they weren by the law,
And doomed for to hang, and draw,
And brent, and with the wind to blow,
That all the world it might know.
And upon this condition
The doom in execution
Was put anon without fail.
And every man hath great marvel
Which heard tellen of this chance,
And thanketh God's purveyance,
Which doth mercy forth with justice.
Slain is the murd'rer, and murd'ress,
Through very truth of righteousness;
And through mercy safe is simplesse[2]
Of her, whom mercy preserveth.
Thus hath he well, that well deserveth."

Dramatis Personæ.—No list of Dramatis Personæ is found in the quartos. It is first given at the end of the play in the 3d folio, where it is headed "The Actors names." Antiochus is there described as "*a Tyrant of* Greece." Then follows "Hesperides *Daughter to* Antiochus." Dionyza is called "Dionysia," and Mytilene "Metaline." Another char-

[1] *Soonde*—gift.

[2] *Simplesse*—simplicity.

acter is introduced, namely, "Philoten *Daughter to* Cleon." The errors and omissions were partly corrected by Rowe and partly by Malone (Camb. ed.).

ACT I.

In the quartos there is no division into acts or scenes. In the folios the acts are marked (the first being headed "*Actus Primus. Scœna Prima*"), but not the scenes.

Gower's Prologue. — 1. *That old.* Steevens reads "of old" (the conjecture of Malone).

2. *Come.* Steevens conjectures "sprung."

6. *Holy-ales.* Rural festivals. Cf. Launce's pun in *T. G. of V.* ii. 5. 61: "to go to the ale with a Christian" (see our ed. p. 136). The early eds. here have "holydayes," "holy dayes," "holy-daies," etc.; corrected by Steevens. A rhyme is evidently required.

7. *In their lives.* Malone changes *in* to "of" (the conjecture of Farmer).

9. *Purchase.* Gain, profit (from reading the tale); changed by Malone to "purpose."

10. *Et bonum*, etc. And a good thing, the older the better. The original saying, as Steevens notes, has "communius" for *antiquius*.

13. *And that.* And if. Gr. 285.

15. *I life would wish*, etc. Mr. Robert Boyle, in his paper "On Wilkins's Share in the Play called Shakspere's *Pericles*" (read before the New Shaks. Soc. March 10, 1882, and printed in the *Transactions*, p. 321 fol.), compares *The Travels of Three English Brothers* (see p. 35 above): "Our lives are lighted tapers that must out."

18. *His chiefest seat.* Steevens quotes Twine (see p. 12 above): "The most famous and mighty King Antiochus, which builded the goodlie city of Antiochia in Syria, and called it after his owne name, as the chiefest seat of all his dominions."

21. *Fere.* Mate, partner; as in *T. A.* iv. 1. 89:

> "the woful fere
> And father of that chaste dishonour'd dame."

Cf. Spenser, *F. Q.* i. 10. 4:

> "But faire Charissa to a lovely fere
> Was lincked, and by him had many pledges dere;"

Id. iv. 3. 52: "And Cambel tooke Cambina to his fere," etc. The early eds. have "peere" or "peer;" corrected by Malone.

23. *Buxom.* Lively, fresh. Cf. *Hen. V.* p. 167.

Full of face. "Completely, exuberantly beautiful" (Malone).

24. *As.* As if. Gr. 107. Cf. i. 1. 16 below.

29. *But custom.* Malone reads "By" for *But*, "perhaps not making sufficient allowance for the inaccurate style" (D.).

30. *Account.* The quartos have "account'd" or "accounted," and the folios "counted." *Account* is the emendation of Malone Cf. Gr. 342.

32. *Thither frame.* "Shape or direct their course thither" (Malone). No similar use of *frame* has been pointed out.

36. *To keep her still*, etc. "To keep her still to himself, and to deter others from demanding her in marriage" (Malone).

39. *A wight.* The folio reading; the quartos have "of wight."

40. *You grim looks.* Referring to the heads of the suitors who had failed to read the riddle, and whose heads were fixed over the palace gate. Cf. Gower's poem, p. 116 above.

41. *Now.* In the first three quartos, but omitted in the other early eds.

42. *Who.* Referring to *judgment.* Gr. 264. For *justify* the folios have "testifie."

SCENE I.—1. *Prince.* As the father of Pericles does not appear to be living, this must be ="prince regnant," as Malone remarks. Twine repeatedly calls him "prince of Tyrus."

6. *Bring in*, etc. The early eds. have "Musicke (or "Musick") bring in," etc. Malone was the first to see that a stage-direction had slipped into the text.

7. *For the.* Fit for the. *The* is not in the early eds., but is due to Malone.

8. *Whose.* Referring, like *her* in the next line, to *daughter.*

For *Lucina* (the goddess who presided over childbirth), cf. iii. 1. 10 below, and *Cymb.* v. 4. 43.

10. *The senate-house*, etc. That is, *that* the planets should sit in council in order to endow her, etc. Steevens quotes Sidney, *Arcadia:* "The senate-house of the planets was at no time so set for the decreeing of perfection in a man," etc.; and Milton, *P. L.* viii. 511:

> "all heaven,
> And happy constellations, on that hour
> Shed their selectest influence."

13. *Graces her subjects*, etc. The Graces being her subjects, and her thoughts the sovereign of every virtue that ennobles humanity.

15. *Her face the book*, etc. "Her face is as a book containing all that is praiseworthy" (Clarke). Malone cites *R. and J.* i. 3. 81:

> "Read o'er the volume of young Paris' face,
> And find delight writ there with beauty's pen;"

Macb. i. 5. 63:

> "Your face, my thane, is as a book, where men
> May read strange matters;"

and *L. L. L.* iv. 2. 113:

> "Study his bias leaves, and make his book thine eyes
> Where all those pleasures live that art could comprehend."

See also *K. John*, ii. 1. 485, *Oth.* iv. 2. 71, etc.

16. *As.* As if. Cf. prol. 24 above. For *raz'd* (Malone's correction) the early eds. have "racte," "rackct," or "rackt."

18. *Her mild companion.* "The companion of her mildness" (Mason). For many similar instances of the use of the adjective, see Schmidt,

p. 1416. H. reads "in her mild company" (the conjecture of Mr. P. A. Daniel).

20. *In my breast.* The folios have "with in" or "within." *Desire* is probably a trisyllable, as Malone makes it. Cf. Gr. 480.

24. *Boundless.* The early eds. all have "bondlesse;" corrected by Rowe.

27. *Hesperides.* That is, Garden of the Hesperides; as in *L. L. L.* iv. 3. 341: "climbing trees in the Hesperides." See our ed. p. 152.

It was probably a misunderstanding of the present passage that led to the insertion of *Hesperides* as the name of the daughter of Antiochus in the *Dramatis Personæ* of the 3d folio. See p. 128 above.

29. *Death-like dragons.* That is, deadly dragons. H. adopts Daniel's reading, "For death, like dragons, here affrights," etc. Walker would read "affront" for *affright.*

31. *Countless.* Infinite. "The poet was probably thinking of the countless eyes of heaven, as he calls them in 73 below" (Malone).

33. *Thy whole heap,* etc. "Thy whole mass must be destroyed. *Thy whole heap,* thy body, must suffer for the offence of a *part,* thine eye" (Malone). The early eds. have "the" for *thy;* corrected by Malone.

34. *Sometimes.* Formerly; changed by Malone to "sometime;" but see *Rich. II.* p. 158.

40. *For.* For fear of. Cf. *T. G. of V.* p. 126, note on *For catching cold.* H. adopts Daniel's conjecture of "met" (="boundary, limit") for *net.*

44. *To what I must.* "That is, to prepare this body for the state to which I must come" (Malone).

46. *Who.* Which. Cf. prol. 42 above.

48. *Who know the world,* etc. "I will act as sick men do; who, having had experience of the pleasures of the world, and only a visionary and distant prospect of heaven, *have neglected the latter for the former;* but *at length* feeling themselves decaying, grasp no longer at temporal pleasures, but prepare calmly for futurity" (Malone).

55–57. *I wait,* etc. The 1st quarto (followed substantially by the others) reads:

> "I wayte the sharpest blow (*Antiochus*)
> Scorning aduice; read the conclusion then:
> Which read," etc.

The folios have:

> "I waite the sharpest blow (*Antiochus*)
> Scorning advice. Reade the conclusion then.
> *Ant.* Which read," etc.

The arrangement in the text is Malone's, and is generally adopted.

59. *Of all say'd.* Of all who have assayed, or made the trial. Cf. the noun *say* in *Lear,* v. 3. 144, and see our ed. p. 255. Mason conjectured "In all, save that, mayst," etc.

62. *Nor ask advice,* etc. As Steevens notes, this is from Sidney's *Arcadia:* "Whereupon asking advice of no other thought but faithfulnesse and courage," etc.

64. *I am no viper,* etc. Mr. R. Boyle (see on i. prol. 15 above) compares *Miseries of Inforced Marriage* (cf. p. 34 above):

> "*John.* He is more degenerate
> Than greedy vipers that devour their mother,
> They eat on her but to preserve themselves.
> *Butler.* But will not suffer
> The husband, viper-like, to prey on them
> That love him, and have cherished him."

70. *They.* The reading in Wilkins's novel is "this," which H. adopts.

72. *Sharp physic is the last.* "That is, the intimation in the last line of the riddle that his life depends on resolving it" (Percy).

73. *Give.* The early eds. have "gives;" corrected by Malone.

74. *Cloud.* The 6th quarto and the folios misprint "could."

87. *Touch not,* etc. "This is a stroke of nature. The incestuous king cannot bear to see a rival touch the hand of the woman he loves. His jealousy resembles that of Antony [*A. and C.* iii. 13, 125]:

> 'to let him be familiar with
> My playfellow, your hand,' etc." (Steevens).

93. *Braid.* Reproach. The verb is found in some old dictionaries—Huloet's, for instance, which has also *braider*=upbraider. Nares quotes the *Mirror for Magistrates:* "And ask forgivenesse for the hastie braid." Many editors follow Malone in printing "'braid."

96. *For vice repeated,* etc. He who reports vicious actions is like the wind, which, while it passes along, blows dust in men's eyes. When it has passed, the eyes, though sore, see clear enough to stop for the future the air that would hurt them.

101. *Copp'd.* "Rising to a top or head" (Steevens). Sandys, in his *Travels*, speaks of "copped caps," and Gascoigne (*Hearbes*) of "high-copt hats." Cf. *T. of S.* p. 167, note on *A copatain hat.* For *throng'd* Steevens reads "wrong'd."

102. *Poor worm.* The mole is so called out of pity. Steevens compares *Temp.* iii. 1. 31: "Poor worm! thou art infected."

107. *First.* Found only in the 1st and 2d quartos.

110. *Gloze.* Use flattery or deceit. Cf. *Rich. II.* ii. 1. 10: "they whom youth and ease have taught to gloze," etc. See also *Hen. V.* p. 146.

111. *Edict.* Accented by Elizabethan writers on either syllable, according to the measure. Cf. *L. L. L.* p. 128.

113. *Cancel of.* The quartos have "counsell of," the folios "cancel off." The text is due to Malone, who is probably right in regarding *cancel* as a noun.

116. *Forty days.* In the old versions of the story, Twine's included, the number is *thirty*.

119. *Entertain.* Not used as a noun by S.

127. *Where.* Whereas. See *T. G. of V.* p. 139, or Gr. 134. For *you're* the quartos all have "you."

129. *Pleasure.* The early eds have "pleasures;" corrected by Rowe.

135. *Blush not.* That is, *who* blush not.

136. *Shun.* The early eds. have "shew;" corrected by Malone.

139. *Sin.* Coll. conjectures "blame," for the sake of the rhyme.

143. *The which.* The early eds. omit *the*, which Malone supplied.

150. *There.* The folios have "here."

152. *Partakes.* Imparts. Cf. *W. T.* p. 214.

163. *Like.* The quarto reading, changed in the folios to "as." Cf. ii. 4. 36 below.

165. *Level.* Aim; as in ii. 3. 114 below. Cf. *Rich. III.* p. 232.

168. *Pistol's length.* For the anachronism cf. 1 *Hen. IV.* p. 169.

SCENE II.—1. *Change of thoughts.* "That change in the disposition of his mind—that unusual propensity to melancholy and cares, which he afterwards describes, and which made his body pine and his soul to languish" (Mason). Malone and Steevens read "charge of thoughts," and the former takes *thoughts* to be = melancholy; a sense which it sometimes has in the singular (cf. *J. C.* p. 146, note on *Take thought, and die*), but rarely, if ever, in the plural. Sr. (2d ed.) reads "charge our thoughts," and St. conjectures "change our thoughts." D., K., and H. adopt Malone's reading.

3. *Be my.* The early eds. have "By me;" corrected by D. (the independent conjecture of V.). *As* = that. See Gr. 109.

8. *Arm.* Changed by D. to "aim." Cf. *T. and C.* ii. 3. 15: "short-armed ignorance;" where some want to read "short-aimed."

15. *Cares it be not done.* "Makes provision that it may not be done" (Malone).

18. *So great can make.* So great that he can make. Gr. 282. Cf. 25 just below.

20. *Honour him.* The early eds. omit *him*, which Rowe supplied.

25. *The ostent.* The display. The early eds. have "the stint;" corrected by Malone (the conjecture of Tyrwhitt). Steevens quotes Dekker, *Entertainment of James I.*, 1604: "And why you bear, alone, th' ostent of warre."

29. *Who am.* The early eds. have "once" for *am*, which was suggested by Farmer.

41. *Heat.* The 1st quarto has "heate," the other early eds. "heart." For *blast* (Mason's conjecture) the early eds. have "sparke" or "spark."

44. *Signior Sooth.* "A near kinsman of this gentleman is mentioned in *W. T.* [i. 2. 196]: 'Sir Smile, his neighbour'" (Malone). Cf. *Rich. II.* p. 196, note on *Words of sooth.*

A peace. The early eds. omit *a*, which was inserted by Malone.

55. *Plants.* The reading of the 1st quarto; "planets" in all the other early eds.

62. *Let their ears hear their faults hid.* "Suffer their ears to hear their failings palliated" (Holt White). D. (followed by W. and H.) changes *hid* to "chid," taking *let* to be = hinder. The emendation is plausible, but not absolutely required.

64. *Mak'st.* The early eds. have "makes." So in 68 below they have "ministers" ("minister's" in 3d folio).

74. *Are arms to princes.* "Such as bring additional strength to princes and joy to their subjects" (Mason). Steevens reads "Bring arms to princes and to subjects joy." W. thinks a line has been lost before this one.

78. *Smooth.* Flatter. Cf. *Rich. III.* pp. 185, 188.

82. *Who.* Which. Cf. i. 1. 46 above.

83. *Bethought me.* The early eds. omit *me*, which is due to Rowe.

86. *Doubt it.* Suspect it, fear it. Cf. i. 3. 19 below, and see *Ham.* p. 187. The first three quartos have "doo't," the other early eds. "thinke" or "think." The emendation was suggested by Steevens, and is confirmed by *lop that doubt* below.

92. *Call 't.* The early eds. have "call" (which the Camb. ed. retains); corrected by Malone.

93. *Spares.* The reading of 1st quarto; "feares" or "fears" in the other early eds.

95. *Reprov'st.* The early eds. have "reprou'dst," "reprovedst" or "reproved'st;" corrected by Malone.

100. *Grieve.* The reading of the 5th quarto; the other early eds. add "for."

116. *Intend.* Schmidt makes this = "bend, direct" (comparing 1 *Hen. IV.* i. 1. 92, *A. and C.* v. 2. 201, etc.); but it may have its ordinary sense.

122. *Orbs.* Spheres. Cf. 1 *Hen. IV.* v. 1. 17:

> "And move in that obedient orb again
> Where you did give a fair and natural light," etc.

See our ed. p. 194.

We 'll. The 1st quarto has "will," the other early eds. "we;" corrected by Malone.

123. *Convince.* Overcome, confute. Cf. *Cymb.* p. 171.

124. *Shine.* For the noun, cf. *V. and A.* 488, 728, and *T. of A.* iii. 5. 101.

SCENE III.—3. *A wise fellow.* "Who this wise fellow was may be known from Barnabie Riche's *Souldier's Wishe to Briton's Welfare*, 1604: 'I will therefore commende the poet Philipides, who being demanded by King Lisimachus, what favour he might doe unto him for that he loved him, made this answere to the king, that your majesty would never impart unto me any of your secrets.'" (Steevens).

7. *Hush.* The early eds. all have "Husht." Cf. *T. of S.* p. 134.

19. *Doubting.* Fearing. See on i. 2. 86 above.

21. *Shipman.* Cf. *T. and C.* v. 2. 172 and *Macb.* i. 3. 17.

22. *Life or death.* The writer doubtless meant that *life or death* was the question *each minute.* H. reads "life with death" (the conjecture of Daniel).

25. *The king's ears it must please.* The early eds. have "the King's Seas must please," which Malone takes to mean "must do their pleasure, must treat him as they will." Percy conjectures "the king it sure must please." K. reads "the king sure must please," and Coll. "the king's ease must please." The text is the conjecture of D. and is adopted by W. and H. It is the best solution of the enigma that has been proposed.

34. *Desire it.* Malone suggested the addition of "told." H. reads "inquire of it" (Walker had conjectured "inquire it").

35. *Commended.* That is, you being commended.

SCENE IV.—8. *Mischief's.* If this be the author's word, it must be used in a subjective sense = "misery's," which H. substitutes (the conjecture of Walker). Steevens reads "mistful," and Sr. "mistie." Malone changes *and seen* to "unseen."

13. *Our tongues and sorrows do sound deep.* H. reads "Our tongues do sound our sorrows and deep woes."

15. *Tongues.* Steevens conjectures "lungs," which Malone and H. adopt. Clarke compares *Rich. II.* i. 3. 173: "Which robs my *tongue* from *breathing* native breath;" and *Id.* i. 3. 257:

> "When the *tongue's* office should be prodigal
> To *breathe* the abundant dolour of the heart."

16. *Heaven.* Changed by Sr. to "the gods;" but cf. *Macb.* ii. 1. 4:

> "There's husbandry in heaven;
> Their candles are all out."

For other instances, see *Rich. II.* p. 157, note on 7.

17. *Helps.* The old eds. have "helpers;" corrected by Malone.

18. *Discourse our woes.* St. conjectures "discourse of woes;" but cf. *M. N. D.* iv. 2. 29: "I am to discourse wonders," etc.

23. *Riches.* Singular, as the word originally was (Fr. *richesse*). Cf. *Sonn.* 87. 6, *Oth.* ii. 1. 83, iii. 3. 173, etc. Steevens would make *Tarsus* the subject of *strew'd*, taking *for riches* to be ="with respect to riches."

26. *Jetted.* Strutted, stalked. Cf. *T. N.* ii. 5. 36: "how he jets under his advanced plumes!" and see our ed. p. 142.

27. *One another's glass.* Cf. 2 *Hen. IV.* ii. 3. 21:

> "he was indeed the glass
> Wherein the noble youth did dress themselves."

See also *Ham.* iii. 1. 161, *Cymb.* i. 1. 49, etc.

34. *Who.* Changed by Malone to "whom." Cf. Gr. 274.

39. *Not yet two summers younger.* The 1st quarto has "not yet two sauers younger," which is repeated essentially by the other early eds. Malone and K. read "us'd to hunger's savour," and W. has "us'd to savour hunger." The text is the conjecture of Mason, and, as the Camb. editors remark, is supported by the following from Wilkins's novel: "The ground of which forced lamentation was, to see the power of change, that this their City, who not two summers younger, did so excell in pompe," etc. The meaning is, "Those palates which, less than two years ago, required some new inventions of cookery to delight their taste, would now be glad of plain bread" (Mason). St. and D. also follow Mason.

42. *Nousle.* Nurse, cherish. See Wb. under *noursle;* and cf. Spenser, *F. Q.* i. 6. 23:

> "Whom, till to ryper years he gan aspyre,
> He nousled up in life and manners wilde;"

Id. v. 1. 6: "In which she noursled him till yeares he raught;" *Id.* vi. 4. 35: "Or noursle up in lore of learn'd Philosophy," etc.

43. *Curious.* Elegant, nice; as in 3 *Hen. VI.* ii. 5. 53: "couched in a curious bed;" *Cymb.* v. 5. 361: "lapp'd In a most curious mantle," etc.

54. *Hear.* Changed by Coll. and H. to "heed." Cf. *Cymb.* iv. 3. 36:

> "I heard no letter from my master since
> I wrote him Imogen was slain."

65. *Nation.* A trisyllable. Gr. 479.

67. *Hath.* The early eds. all have "That;" corrected by Rowe.

69. *Unhappy me.* Malone changes *me* to "men" (so H.), and Steevens conjectures "we."

70. *Whereas.* Where. Cf. 2 *Hen. VI.* p. 153. For the use of the infinitive in *to overcome*, see Gr. 356.

71. *Semblance.* A trisyllable. Gr. 477.

74. *Like him 's.* "Like him who is;" which Steevens was inclined to read, making *Thou speak'st* a separate line. For *him 's* the early eds. have "himmes," "hymmes," "hymnes," "hymns," etc.

83. *Consist.* "Stand" (Malone). Schmidt makes it ="insist." Cf. 2 *Hen. IV.* p. 183.

92. *Happily.* Haply. See *T. N.* p. 158, or Gr. 42.

93. *Was stuff'd.* Which was stuffed. Some editors adopt Steevens's conjecture of "war-stuff'd."

94. *Veins.* Malone has "views" (proposed by Steevens), and Coll. conjectures "bones." *Expecting overthrow* refers to *you.*

98. *Arise.* Changed by Steevens to "Rise." For *rise*, all the early eds. but the 1st quarto have "arise," which Rowe adopts.

102. *In thought.* Even in thought. Malone conjectures "in aught."

ACT II.

GOWER'S PROLOGUE.—2. *I wis.* I know. See *M. of V.* p. 146.

3. *Benign.* Accented on the first syllable. The word does not occur in S.

4. *Awful.* Full of awe, reverent, or "conscientious" (Schmidt). Cf. *T. G. of V.* p. 145.

7. *I'll show you those*, etc. "I will now exhibit to you persons who, after suffering small and temporary evils, will at length be blessed with happiness" (Malone). The title of the chapter in the *Gesta Romanorum* in which the story of Appolinus is told is "De tribulatione temporali quae in gaudium sempiternum postremo commutabitur."

9. *Conversation.* Conduct. Cf. *A. and C.* p. 189, or 2 *Hen. IV.* p. 205. Steevens cites 2 *Peter*, iii. 11. Gower means to say "The good prince (on whom I bestow my best wishes) is still at Tarsus, where every man," etc.

12. *Thinks all is writ.* Probably =thinks all is as holy writ.

Speken. The early eds. all have "spoken;" corrected by W. *Speken* is an obsolete form of *speak.* Cf. *killen* in 20 below.

14. *Build.* Steevens would read "Gild," quoting Gower's description of the statue: "It was of laton over-gylte."

19. *Though he strive.* The early eds. have "for though," for which Steevens conjectures "forth" (="thoroughly," for which meaning he thinks he finds authority in *M. for M.* v. 1. 255), and Sr. and W. read "for-thy" (=therefore). H. is probably right in dropping "for," but we cannot accept his interpretation of *though*, which he makes ="since,

for, because" (cf. *T. of A.* p. 164), though we have no better one to suggest. It is a sufficient objection to the emendations of Steevens and Sr. that they would require *strives* rather than *strive.*

21. *Prince'.* The early eds. have "prince" or "princes." Malone is doubtless right in considering the word one of the contracted possessives not unfrequently found in S. Cf. *Rich. III.* i. 4. 191: "poor Clarence' death," etc. See also Gr. 471.

22. *Sends word.* The early eds. have "Sau'd one" or "Sav'd one." The emendation (which Halliwell says was suggested to Steevens by a MS. note of Theobald's) is confirmed by Wilkins's novel: "Good Helycanus as prouident at home, as his Prince was prosperous abroade, let no occasion slip wherein hee might *send word* to Tarsus of what occurrents soeuer had happened in his absence," etc.

27. *Doing so.* "That is, as Helicanus recommended" (W.). Steevens conjectures "knowing so," which K. and H. adopt.

28. *Been.* Archaic for *are.* Most of the early eds. have "bin," a common spelling in old writers.

32. *Wrack'd.* All the early eds. have "wrackt." Cf. *Cymb.* p. 177. Note the rhyme in iv. prol. 11, 12 below.

36. *Escapen.* The early eds. have "escapend" or "escapen'd;" corrected by Steevens (the conjecture of Percy). See on 12 above. *Ne*= nor, as often in Old English.

38. *Give him glad.* Percy conjectures "make" for *give;* but the expression is doubtless meant to be an archaism. Steevens remarks: "The language of our fictitious Gower is so often irreconcilable to the practice of any age that criticism on such bungling imitations is almost thrown away."

40. *This longs the text.* This belongs to the text. Even here some editors print "'longs." See Wb., or *Hen. VIII.* p. 162.

SCENE I.—*Pentapolis.* One of the names given to the district of North Africa otherwise known as Cyrenaica. It is found in all the old versions of the story.

6. *Me breath.* The early eds. have "my breath;" corrected by Malone.

12. *What, ho, Pilch!* The early eds. have "what, to pelch?" The correction is Malone's. *Pilch* meant a leathern coat, and is put for the wearer, like *Patch-breech* just below.

17. *Wanion.* "Used only in the phrase *with a wanion*, but totally unexplained, though exceedingly common in use; seemingly =with a vengeance, or with a plague" (Nares).

20. *Alas, poor souls,* etc. Cf. *W. T.* iii. 3. 91 fol.: "O, the most piteous cry of the poor souls!" etc.

23. *Porpus.* Porpoise; spelt "porpas" in all the early eds. The notion that the appearance of porpoises forebodes a storm is very old. Malone quotes Webster, *Duchess of Malfi:* "He lifts his nose like a foul porpus before a storm."

27. *A-land.* Steevens says that the word occurs several times in Twine's novel. The hyphen is found only in the 1st quarto. Cf. iii. 2. 69 below.

The great ones eat up the little ones. Mr. R. Boyle (see on i. prol. 15 above) compares Wilkins's *Miseries of Inforced Marriage:*

> "These men, like fish, do swim within one stream,
> Yet they 'd eat one another;"

and Day's *Law Tricks* (in which he thinks Wilkins had a share), i. 2:

> "*Joculo.* But, madam, do you remember what a multitude of fishes we saw at sea: and I do wonder how they can all live by one another.
> *Emilia.* Why, fool, as men do on the land; the great ones eat up the little ones."

Again, in the same play, we find:

> "*Adam.* I knew one of that faculty in one term eat up a whole town, church, steeple, and all.
> *Julio.* I wonder the bells rung not all in his belly."

44. *Finny.* The early eds. have "fenny." The correction was suggested by Steevens, and is supported by Wilkins's novel: "Prince Pericles wondering that from the finny subjects of the sea these poore country people learned the infirmities of men."

49. *If it be a day fits you, search,* etc. The text is doubtless corrupt, and has been variously emended. Malone reads "scratch it" (the conjecture of Steevens) for *search*, and H. adopts the anonymous conjecture "steal't." Clarke thinks the meaning may be "search *it* out" (that is, "with intention to take"), and nobody "*will* look after it." Farmer thinks that in *honest* there may be an allusion to the *dies honestissimus* of Cicero. Malone remarks: "Some difficulty, however, will remain, unless we suppose a preceding line to have been lost; for Pericles has said nothing about the *day.* I suspect that in the lost line he wished the men a *good day.*" K., who retains the old text, asks: "Does it not mean that the fisherman, laughing at the rarity of being honest, remarks, If it be a day (that is, a saint's or red-letter day) fits you, search out of (not *in*) the calendar, and nobody look after it (there, as it would be useless)?"

51. *You may see,* etc. The quartos read: "May see the sea hath cast upon your coast;" and the folios: "Y' may see the sea hath cast me upon your coast." The text is due to Malone (ed. 1780), but he afterwards adopted the conjecture of Steevens: "Nay, see, the sea hath cast upon your coast—;" the sentence being continued, after the interruption by the fisherman, with "A man whom," etc. W. believes that "a speech, or more, preceding this one has been lost."

55. *In that vast tennis-court,* etc. Boyle quotes *The Travels of the Three English Brothers* (see p. 35 above):

> "Think that the seas
> Play'd with us but as great men die a-land,
> Hurl'd us now up, now down."

Steevens compares Sidney, *Arcadia:* "In such a shadow . . . mankind lives, that neither they know how to foresee, nor what to feare, and are, like tenis bals, tossed by the racket of the higher powers."

For *hath made*, the reading of all the early eds., and probably a "confusion of construction" on the part of the writer, D. reads "have made."

66. *Throng'd up.* "Filled completely, possessed entirely" (Schmidt);

or "hard pressed, beset" (Clarke). Cf. i. 1. 101 above. Steevens conjectures "shrunk up."

71. *Quoth-a.* The early eds. all have "ke-tha;" corrected by Malone.

72. *Afore me.* By my life, on my soul. Cf. *R. and J.* iii. 4. 34: "Afore me, it is so very late," etc.

73. *Holidays.* The early eds. have "all day;" corrected by Malone. Mason conjectures "all-days."

74. *Moreo'er.* Farmer's correction of the "more; or" of the early eds.

Flap-jacks. Pancakes. The word is obsolete in England, though in familiar use in New England. It is not used by S.

82. *O, not all.* Walker conjectures "O, no, not all."

88. *Pentapolis.* The quartos spell it "Pantapoles," and the folios "Pantapolis."

98. *Just.* Tilt. Cf. the noun in *Rich II.* v. 2. 52.

102. *What a man cannot get,* etc. The meaning seems to be that "what a man cannot accomplish he may lawfully endeavour to obtain" (Mason); but what *his wife's soul* has to do with it is not so clear. As K. remarks, "there are more riddles in this play than that of Antiochus." Clarke explains it thus: "A man who has not much chance of getting his wife's soul out of purgatory may nevertheless pay for masses with that view." Steevens conjectures that *His wife's soul* begins a new sentence, which is interrupted by the next speaker. We are inclined to agree with W. that something has probably been lost.

105. *Bots on 't!* A comic execration found in sundry old writers. Percy quotes the ballad of *The Miller of Mansfield:* "Quoth Dick, a bots on you!"

108. *Thy crosses.* The early eds. omit *thy,* which Delius supplied from Wilkins's novel. Malone reads "my."

110. *And though.* Walker conjectures "An though." "I thank you" is understood before *though,* being implied in *Thanks, fortune.*

114. *Brace.* Armour for the arm. Cf. its figurative use in *Oth.* i. 3. 24: "in such warlike brace." We find *vantbrace* in *T. and C.* i. 3. 297. See our ed. p. 175.

116. *The which,* etc. Steevens reads "Which gods protect thee from! —it may," etc. The early eds. have "thee, Fame may" for *thee from!— 't may,* which is the reading of Malone. The Camb. ed. has "from!— may defend thee."

118. *Spare.* The early eds. have "spares;" corrected by Malone.

129. *Fortune's better.* The reading of the early eds. Some editors adopt Mason's conjecture of "fortunes better," making *better* a verb.

133. *Do 'e.* The reading of the 1st quarto. The 2d and 3d quartos have "di 'e," and the other early eds. omit it. Malone reads "do ye."

137. *Condolements.* Blunderingly used by the fisherman—perhaps somehow confused with *dole* (=share, portion), for which see *W. T.* p. 156.

Vails is explained by Schmidt as "money given to servants" (cf. Wb.), but it was also =avails. Some print "'vails" here.

138. *Had it.* The early eds. have "had them;" corrected by Malone

140. *Furtherance.* Assistance; a good word enough, though Steevens wanted to read "forbearance."

141. *Rapture.* Violent seizure (the etymological sense), robbery. The early eds. have "rupture;" but Rowe's emendation is confirmed by Wilkins's novel: "a jewel, whom all the raptures of the sea could not bereave from his arm."

142. *Building.* A suspicious word, though it may possibly be =firm position, fixed place, as some explain it. Malone at first changed it to "gilding," but later he adopted Steevens's conjecture of "biding." "Binding" has also been suggested. *His*=its; as often. For *jewel*, cf. *T. N.* p. 154.

143. *Unto thy value.* That is, according to it. Walker would change *thy* to "the." He asks, "Why should he apostrophize the jewel?" Clarke aptly replies that "he does so in the sudden gladness of discovering that he still possesses this resource wherewith to purchase the horse he needs for the tournament."

147. *Bases.* "A kind of embroidered mantle which hung down from the middle to about the knees or lower, worn by knights on horseback" (Nares). It must of course have consisted of two parts—a double skirt, perhaps. Steevens quotes Sidney, *Arcadia:* "About his middle he had, instead of bases, a long cloake of silke," etc. Mason adds, from Massinger's *Picture:* "Your petticoat serves for bases to this warrior.

150. *A goal to.* D. conjectures "but goal unto," and St. "equal to."

SCENE II.—1. *Triumph.* Tournament. See the long note in *T. G. of V.* p. 153.

4. *Our daughter.* The early eds. add "heere" or "here," which Malone struck out.

14. *Interpret.* The early eds. have "entertaine" or "entertain." Many editors adopt Steevens's conjecture of "explain" (a word, by the by, not found in S.), but Schmidt's suggestion of *interpret* is more plausible.

For *honour* (=honourable duty or office), Steevens conjectures "office."

21. *Lux tua vita mihi.* Thy light is my life. *Word*=motto.

27. *Piu por dulzura,* etc. More by gentleness than by force. The *piu* is Italian, the corresponding Spanish being *mas.* The two languages were much confused by the old writers. The early eds. print the motto thus: "Pue Per doleera kee per forsa." In Wilkins's novel it reads: "Pue per dolcera qui per sforsa." All the other mottos are Latin.

30. *Me pompae provexit apex.* The crown of honour has led me on; or "the desire of renown drew me to this enterprise" (Wilkins). The early eds. all have "Pompey" for *pompae,* which was suggested by Steevens and is confirmed by Wilkins's novel.

33. *Quod me alit, me extinguit.* That which feeds me extinguishes me; or "that which gives me life gives me death" (Wilkins). The early eds. have "Qui" for *Quod,* which is due to Malone.

34. *His.* Its. Walker conjectures "her." Cf. ii. 1. 142 above.

38. *Sic spectanda fides.* So faith is to be tested; or "so faith is to be looked into" (Wilkins).

42. *Present.* That which he *presents* or bears as a device. Sr. changes it to "impress."

44. *In hac spe vivo.* In this hope I live.

49. *Commend.* Used by S. as a noun only in the plural. See *Rich. II.* p. 188.

51. *The whipstock.* "That is, the carter's whip" (Steevens).

56. *Opinion.* Public opinion, reputation. See 1 *Hen. IV.* p. 179.

57. *The outward habit*, etc. That is, the inward man by the outward dress. For examples of somewhat similar inversions, see Schmidt, p. 1424. Steevens would transpose *outward* and *inward*.

SCENE III.—3. *To place.* The reading of the 4th folio; "I place" in all the other early eds.

15. *An artist.* Changed by Steevens to "artists" (the conjecture of Malone).

19. *Marshal.* All the early eds. have "Martiall" or "Martial;" corrected by Malone.

28, 29. *By Jove . . . upon.* Steevens would give these lines to Pericles, changing *he* to "she;" but Wilkins's novel shows that they belong to Simonides, as in the early eds.: "As it were by some divine operation, both king and daughter at one instant were so strucke in love with the noblenesse of his woorth, that they could not spare so much time to satisfie themselves with the delicacie of their viands, for talking of his prayses."

Cates. Dainties, delicacies. Cf. the play on the word in *T. of S.* ii. 1. 190: "For dainties are all Kates."

Resist me. "Go against my stomach" (Steevens), are distasteful to me.

He not thought upon. Some editors adopt Mason's conjecture of "but" for *not;* but the old text may be explained as by K.: "Simonides wonders that he cannot eat although he (Pericles) is *not thought upon.* This is an attempt to disguise the cause of his solicitude even to himself. It must be observed that the succeeding speeches of Simonides, Thaisa, and Pericles are all to be received as soliloquies. In the second speech, Simonides continues the idea of *he not thought upon* by attempting to depreciate Pericles—'He 's but a country gentleman.'" V., D., and the Camb. editors also retain *not*, though D. is inclined to favour "but."

30. *Marriage.* A trisyllable. Cf. *T. of S.* p. 152.

34. *Has.* For the ellipsis of the subject, cf. Gr. 400.

42. *Vail.* Lower, let fall. See *M. of V.* p. 128. Cf. iv. prol. 29 below.

43. *Where.* Whereas; as in i. 1. 127 above. For *son's* the early eds. have "sonne," "sunne," or "son;" corrected by Malone.

46. *For he 's.* The first three quartos have "He 's but;" the other early eds. read as here.

50. *Stor'd.* The early eds. have "stur'd," "sturd," or "stirr'd." The emendation is due to Steevens.

64. *Are wonder'd at.* "That is, when they are found to be such small insignificant animals, after making so great a noise" (Percy). "The worthless monarch and the idle gnat have only lived to make an empty bluster; and when both alike are dead, we wonder how it happened that

they made so much, or that we permitted them to make it" (Steevens). H. adopts Daniel's over-ingenious emendation, "but still ne'er wonder'd at."

64. *Entrance.* A trisyllable; as in *R. and J.* i. 4. 8. Gr. 477. The folios have "entrance now." H. adopts Walker's suggestion of "entertain."

65. *Standing-bowl.* "A bowl resting on a foot" (Steevens).

73. *And furthermore,* etc. Malone reads: "And further tell him, we desire to know, Of whence," etc.

82. *My education been.* The 5th quarto has "being" for *been*, and Sr. conjectures "'s been;" but Wilkins's novel has "his name Pericles; his education beene in artes and armes," etc.

87–89. Malone "fixes up" the passage thus:

"A gentleman of Tyre, who only by
Misfortune of the sea has been bereft
Of ships and men, and cast upon this shore."

94. *Address'd.* Prepared; as often. See *J. C.* p. 156, or *M. N. D.* p. 182.

95. *A soldier's dance.* Malone says: "The dance here introduced is thus described in an ancient 'Dialogue against the Abuse of Dancing' (black letter, no date):

'There is a dance call'd Choria,
Which joy doth testify;
Another call'd Pyrricke
Which warlike feats doth try.
For men in armour gestures made,
And leap'd, that so they might
When need requires, be more prompt
In public weal to fight.'"

97. *Loud music.* "The loud music made by the clashing of their armour" (Malone).

101. *Breathing.* Exercise. Cf. *Ham.* p. 272, note on *Breathing time.*

102. *Have heard.* Malone reads "have often heard."

114. *Level.* Aim; as in i. 1. 165 above.

116. *Speeding.* Achieving success.

SCENE IV.—3–10. In the early eds. the lines of this corrupt passage end with *minding, that, heinous, pride, seated in, daughter, shrivell'd,* and *stunk.* The modern editors have arranged them in various ways. We give 3–6 as Malone has them, and 7–10 as D. does.

10. *Their.* The early eds. have "those;" corrected by Steevens, and confirmed by Wilkins's novel.

13–15. Arranged as by Malone. In the early eds. the lines end with *great, shaft,* and *reward.*

19. *Grieve.* Grieve or offend us.

23. *Griefs.* Grievances. Cf. 1 *Hen. IV.* p. 192.

31. *Resolv'd.* Satisfied; as in ii. 5. 68 below. Cf. *J. C.* p. 158.

32. *Gives.* All the early eds. but the 5th quarto have "give's" (give us), which the Camb. ed. retains.

34. *The strongest in our censure.* "The most probable in our opinion" (Steevens). For *censure*, cf. *Ham.* p. 190.

36. *Like.* As. See on i. 1. 163 above. Malone makes the line a parenthesis, and reads "Soon will fall to ruin," which Steevens changes to "Will soon to ruin fall."

38. *Know.* The reading of the first two quartos; "knowes" or "knows" in the other early eds. Malone reads "know'st."

41. *For honour's cause.* The early eds. have "Try" instead of *For*, which was proposed by D.

43. *Seas.* That is, a sea of difficulty. Malone reads "seat."

45. *Entreat you.* Steevens reads "then entreat," and H. "you entreat."

46. *To forbear.* To bear, or bear with. H. reads "Still to forbear" (an anonymous conjecture).

50. *Nobles.* Steevens reads "noblemen."

56. *Endeavour it.* Steevens supplied *it*, which is wanting in the early eds. The Globe ed. has "endeavour us."

Scene V.—2. *This I let you know*, etc. Clarke remarks: "The expedient here devised by Simonides for having the suitors 'well despatch'd' is indeed not very consonant with the dignity of truth; but it is quite characteristic of the waggish tendency to stratagem shown by the royal old gentleman, in proceeding to 'dissemble' his satisfaction at his daughter's choice, and to play off a pretended anger at the lovers' mutual affection, that he may keep them in a flutter of suspense until he choose to join their hands and bid them wed at once as the penalty of their transgression, in daring to fall in love without his leave. Steevens solemnly demurs to this conduct of Simonides; yet, though it may not be 'ingenuous,' it is perfectly in character—diplomatically as well as dramatically."

13. *Loath.* Steevens reads "Though loath."

17. *To view.* For the *to*, see Gr. 350.

18. *'T is well, mistress.* Steevens has "Mistress, 't is well."

25. *Beholding.* Changed by Malone to "beholden," which is not found in S. See *M. of V.* p. 135.

34. *A most.* Steevens reads: "As of a most."

39. *And she will be your scholar.* Steevens reads: "And she 'll your scholar be."

52. *Levy.* A strange use of the word, though intelligible enough.

62. *Her.* The 5th quarto has "our," and Walker suggests "your."

68. *Resolve.* Satisfy, inform. See on ii. 4. 31 above.

71. *Say.* Found only in the 1st quarto.

87. *A further.* The early eds. omit *a*, which Malone supplied.

89. *My life, or blood.* The early quartos have "my life my blood."

92. *That I will.* Malone reads "that I 'll," and Steevens "I 'll."

93. *And then.* Steevens omitted *And.* He also remarks here: "I cannot dismiss the foregoing scene till I have expressed the most supreme contempt of it. Such another gross, nonsensical dialogue would be sought for in vain among the earliest and rudest efforts of the British theatre. It is impossible not to wish that the Knights had horsewhipped Simonides, and that Pericles had kicked him off the stage."

ACT III.

GOWER'S PROLOGUE.—1. *Yslaked.* For the old participial prefix *y-*, see Gr. 345. Cf. 35 below.

2. *The house about.* The early eds. have "about the house;" corrected by Malone.

3. *Breast.* All the early eds. except the first three quartos misprint "beast."

5. *Eyne.* This old plural is often used by S. for the sake of the rhyme (see *T. of S.* p. 168), and in *R. of L.* 1229 independently of the rhyme.

6. *Fore.* The early eds. have "from;" corrected by Malone.

8. *E'er.* The early eds. have "Are," for which Malone reads "As," and D. "Aye." *E'er* was a conjecture of D. first put in the text by Sr. Clarke retains "Are;" and the ellipsis is not unlike many in these Gower passages.

13. *Eche.* An old spelling of *eke.* Cf. *Hen. V.* p. 162, note on *Eke. Quaintly*=skilfully. Cf. *T. G. of V.* p. 131.

14. *Plain.* Make plain, explain.

15. *Dern.* "Lonely, solitary, melancholy" (Steevens and Wb.); or "dreadful" (Schmidt). Some make it ="earnest, eager." It seems to be found in old writers in all these senses. It is often spelt *dearn.*

Perch is doubtless the measure of length (=rod), but some have thought it to be =resting-place.

17. *Coigns.* Corners. See *Macb.* p. 174. The early eds. have "crignes;" corrected by Rowe.

21. *Stead the quest.* Aid the search; cf. iv. prol. 41 below; and see *M. of V.* p. 133, note on *May you stead me?*

27. *Set on.* For the double preposition, see Gr. 407.

29. *Oppress.* Suppress, put down. Steevens reads "appease."

32. *Dooms.* Judgments. Cf. v. 2. 20 below.

35. *Yravished.* The 1st quarto has "Iranyshed," the 2d "Irany shed," and the other early eds. "Irony shed;" corrected by Steevens. See on 1 above.

36. *Can.* An old form of *gan* (=began). See *L. L. L.* p. 149, note on 101.

46. *Fortune's mood.* The early eds. have "fortune mou'd" ("moou'd" or "mov'd"); corrected by Steevens.

47. *Grisly.* Terrible. The 1st quarto has "grisled;" the other early eds. "grislee" or *grisly.* See *M. N. D.* p. 183.

51. *Well-a-near.* "Well-a-day" (which Wilkins gives instead); a provincial interjection.

53. *Fell.* The reading of the 1st quarto; "selfe" or "self" in the other early eds. V. takes *fell* to be a corruption of the modern editors, and reads "self."

55. *Nill.* Will not. Cf. *Ham.* p. 259.

60. *Sea-tost.* The early eds. have "seas tost;" corrected by Rowe.

SCENE I.—"The diction throughout the present scene is veritably Shakespearian. It has that majesty of unrestrained force which distinguishes his finest descriptive passages, and that dignity of expression, combined with the most simple and natural pathos, which characterizes his passages of deepest passion. After the comparative stiffness traceable in the phraseology of the previous scenes, and after the cramped and antiquated chant-speeches of Gower, this opening of the 3d act always comes upon us with the effect of a grand strain of music—the music of the great master himself—with its rightly touched discords and its nobly exalted soul-sufficing harmonies" (Clarke).

1. *Thou.* The early eds. have "The;" corrected by Rowe.

4. *Call'd.* Fleay reads "recall'd," which may be right.

5. *Deafening.* The first three quartos have "deafning," the other early eds. "dearning." For *gently*, the reading of 1st quarto, the other early eds. have "dayly" or "daily."

6. *Nimble, sulphurous flashes.* Cf. *Lear*, ii. 4. 167 (see also iv. 7. 34): "You nimble lightnings," etc.

7. *Thou stormest venomously.* The early eds. have "then storme venomously," and Malone reads "Thou storm, venomously." The text is due to D. Clarke objects to it that it "destroys the address to the storm;" but it merely changes the form of the address, and seems to us more like Shakespeare than Malone's reading, which Clarke adopts.

Pericles is on the deck, Lychorida in the cabin. He goes on to say that the noise of the storm drowns even the boatswain's whistle; and his thought seems to be, "How then can Lychorida hear me?" He repeats the cry more loudly, but still getting no response lapses into prayer for Thaisa.

8. *Spet.* An obsolete spelling of *spit*, for which see *M. of V.* p. 135. Here the quartos have "speat" and the 3d folio "spet," for which the 4th folio substitutes "spit."

11. *Midwife.* The early eds. have "my wife;" corrected by Steevens.

14. *Travail.* The early eds. have "travails;" corrected by D. S. elsewhere uses the singular. Clarke, who retains "travails," compares the plural in *Rich. III.* iv. 1. 24: "Then bring me to their sights;" but there, as in many similar instances, it is used because more than one person is referred to. Cf. *Rich. II.* p. 206, note on *Sights*.

16. *Conceit.* Ability to *conceive*, or think. Cf. 2 *Hen. IV.* ii. 4. 263: "there's no more conceit in him than is in a mallet," etc.

19. *Do not assist the storm.* Cf. *Temp.* i. 1. 15: "You do assist the storm."

26. *Vie honour with you.* Contend with you in honour. Cf. iv. prol. 33 below. The early eds. have "vse" for *vie*, which was suggested by Mason.

29. *Conditions.* Qualities, disposition. Cf. *M. of V.* p. 133.

30. *Welcome.* Changed by Malone to "welcom'd;" but the text is supported by Wilkins's novel: "Poor inch of nature! quoth he, thou art as rudely welcome to the world, as ever princess' babe was," etc. "Poor inch of nature!" seems like a bit of Shakespeare somehow lost from the text.

32. *Chiding.* Noisy. Cf. *M. N. D.* p. 175.

35. *Thy loss,* etc. "Thou hast already lost more (by the death of thy mother) than thy safe arrival at the port of life can counterbalance, with all to boot that we can give thee" (Steevens). For *quit*=requite, see *Ham.* p. 269, or *Rich. II.* p. 208.

39. *Flaw.* Gust, blast. See *Ham.* p. 264.

43. *Bolins.* Bowlines; used by S. only here. We find it in *Two Noble Kinsmen,* iv. 1 (Fletcher's part): "Top the bowling; out with the mainsail!"

45. *But sea-room,* etc. Cf. *Temp.* i. 1. 8: "Blow till thou burst thy wind, if room enough!"

51. *Still.* Ever, constantly; as very often. Gr. 69.

The 1st quarto (followed substantially by the other early eds.) arranges the context thus:

> "1. Pardon vs, sir; with vs at Sea it hath bin still obserued.
> And we are strong in easterne, therefore briefly yeeld'er.
> *Per.* As you thinke meet; for she must over board straight:
> Most wretched Queene."

Malone was the first to read the whole as prose, and to transfer *for she must overboard straight* to the Sailor's speech.

Custom for "easterne" was suggested by Boswell. Mason conjectured "earnest," and Steevens "credence." K. adopts Jackson's conjecture: "And we are strong in, astern."

55. *Here she lies.* Here we must suppose that a curtain is drawn aside, the space behind which represents the cabin below. This was all that the rude appliances of the old stage permitted; the spectator's imagination had to supply the rest.

60. *In the ooze.* The early eds. have "in oare" or "in oar;" corrected by Steevens. Cf. *Temp.* iii. 3. 10: "my son i' the ooze is bedded."

61. *For.* Instead of. Gr. 148.

62. *Aye-remaining.* The early eds. have "ayre remayning," "ayre remaining," or "air remaining;" corrected by Malone.

63. *And humming water,* etc. See p. 38 above. Cf. *Lycidas,* 157: "where thou perhaps under the humming tide," etc.

67. *Coffer.* The early eds. have "coffin;" corrected by Malone. Pericles would not have carried a *coffin* to sea with him. The ancient coffers were often lined with *satin* or other costly material. *Satin coffer* may, however, as some suppose, be a chest in which satins were kept. The *chest* mentioned just below was probably (as Clarke suggests) intended as an outer case for the *coffer.*

75. *Alter thy course for Tyre.* That is, which is *now* for Tyre. Coll. conjectures "from Tyre," as in Wilkins's novel.

81. *Presently.* At once. Cf. *M. of V.* p. 131.

SCENE II.—9. *Pothecary.* A common form of *apothecary.* See *R. and J.* p. 218.

The recipe, as Malone notes, must be for the poor men already mentioned, or for the servant himself. It is evident that it cannot be for his master.

16. *Principals.* Corner-posts, main timbers.

17. *All to topple.* Some print "all-to topple," and others "all to-topple;" but the *all* may refer to *principals*, or it may be an adverb used intensively, as often. Cf. *M. W.* p. 160 (note on *To-pinch*) and *K. John*, p. 173 (on *To spend*).

20. *Husbandry.* Thrift, economy (here of time). Cf. *Macb.* p. 183.

22. *Tire.* Apparently =furniture. The early eds. except the first three quartos have "attire." Steevens conjectures "such towers" for *rich tire.*

Petty. The reading of the first three quartos; "pretty" in the other early eds.

26. *Held.* The early eds. have "hold;" but the following *were* favours Malone's emendation.

27. *Cunning.* Knowledge, wisdom. Cf. *Cor.* p. 249, or *Oth.* p. 183. See also p. 38 above.

36. *Vegetives.* Vegetables; used by S. only here.

37. *I can.* The early eds. omit *I*, which Malone supplied.

41. *Treasure.* The early eds. have "pleasures" or "pleasure;" corrected by Steevens.

42. *The fool and death.* Malone thought that this alludes to the old moralities; but the reference is probably to the pictures of the "Dance of Death." Steevens mentions an old Flemish print, in which Death is represented as plundering a miser of his bags, while the fool stands grinning behind. V. remarks: "The 'Dance of Death' appears to have been anciently a popular exhibition. A venerable and aged clergyman informed Steevens that he had once been a spectator of it. The dance consisted of Death's contrivances to surprise the Merry Andrew, and of the Merry Andrew's efforts to elude the stratagems of Death, by whom at last he was overpowered; his finale being attended with such circumstances as mark the exit of the Dragon of Wantley. It should seem that the general idea of this serio-comic *pas-de-deux* had been borrowed from the ancient 'Danse de Macabre,' commonly called the 'Dance of Death,' which appears to have been anciently acted in churches, like the moralities. The subject was a frequent ornament of cloisters, both here and abroad. The reader will remember the beautiful series of wood-cuts of the 'Dance of Death,' attributed (though erroneously) to Holbein. Douce describes an exquisite set of initial letters, representing the same subject; in one of which the Fool is engaged in a very stout combat with his adversary, and is actually buffeting him with a bladder filled with peas or pebbles—an instrument used by modern Merry Andrews."

48. *Time shall never raze.* The first three quartos have "time shall never." The other early eds. read "as never shall decay." Malone prints "time shall never—" St. reads "time shall ne'er decay." The text is due to D. *Raze* is favoured by the preceding *built.*

51. *Wrack.* See on ii. prol. 32 above.

56. *Bitum'd.* The early eds. have "bottomed," "bottomd," or "bottom'd;" corrected by Malone, and supported by Wilkins's novel. Cf. also iii. 1. 71 above.

67. *Apollo, perfect me,* etc. May Apollo enable me to decipher it!

69. *A-land.* See on ii. 1. 27 above.

77. *Cracks.* Cf. *M. W.* ii. 2. 301: "my heart is ready to crack," etc. See also *Ham.* v. 2. 370.

84. *I heard*, etc. The passage is probably corrupt, as Wilkins's novel makes *Egyptian* refer to those who recovered the apparently dead: "I have read of some Egyptians, who after four houres death (if a man may call it so) have raised impoverished bodies, like to this, unto their former health." Malone and Steevens read "I have heard," etc.

85. *Lien.* The reading of the first three quartos; "bene," "beene," or "been" in the other early eds. Cf. *K. John*, p. 163.

86. *By good appliance recovered.* The reading of all the early eds. Steevens reads (omitting *Who*), "By good appliance was recovered." D. has "appliances recover'd." For the singular *appliance*, cf. *A. W.* ii. 1. 116, *Hen. VIII.* i. 1. 124, and *Ham.* iv. 3. 10. S. uses the plural only in 2 *Hen. IV.* iii. 1. 29 and *M. for M.* iii. 1. 89.

87. *Well said.* Well done; as often. Cf. *Oth.* p. 174.

90. *Vial.* The early quartos have "violl;" the later ones and the folios "viall" or "vial." The modern editors are divided between *vial* and "viol." W. remarks: "Cerimon's call for music might lead us to suppose that we should read *viol*, were it not that he has but just issued the order, and so would not say 'the viol *once more*.'" It might be replied that *once more* is perhaps $=$*I say* once more. Clarke puts the case for *vial* better, we think: "It is more likely that he should be eager to have some pungent essence for Thaisa to inhale, than that he should name some special instrument when desiring that *music* shall play. It appears to us that the call for music is made and renewed; while the demand for *the vial* is parenthetical."

93. *Awakes*, etc. The 1st quarto has "awakes a warmth breath;" the other early eds. "awakes a warme breath." The correction is due to Steevens.

95. *Gins.* Commonly printed "'gins;" but see *Macb.* p. 153.

99. *Cases.* Cf. *W. T.* v. 2. 14 and *Lear*, iv. 6. 147.

103. *Do.* The early eds. have "doth;" corrected, perhaps unnecessarily, by Malone. Cf. Gr. 334.

SCENE III.—3. *Litigious.* The word is found only in the first three quartos.

6. *Shafts.* The early eds. have "shakes," and for *hurt* "hant," "haunt," or "hate;" corrected by Steevens.

7. *Wanderingly.* The early eds. have "wondringly;" also corrected by Steevens.

13. *For.* Because. Gr. 151.

19. *Still.* Constantly; as in iii. 1. 51 above. All the early eds. except the 1st quarto have "dayly" or "daily."

20. *Neglection.* The reading of the first three quartos; "neglect" in the other early eds. Cf. *T. and C.* i. 3. 127: "neglection of degree."

29. *Unscissar'd shall this hair*, etc. The early eds. have "unsisterd shall this heyre" ("his heyres" in the 5th quarto); corrected by Steevens, and confirmed by Wilkins's novel.

30. *Ill.* The early eds. have "will." The correction, according to the Camb. ed., was suggested by Malone, and adopted by Sr. (2d ed.); but D. says: "The reading *show ill* is mine, and has been adopted by Mr. Collier in his 2d edition, by Mr. Staunton, by Mr. Grant White, and by the Cambridge editors (Globe ed.)." It is also in their Camb. ed.

36. *Mask'd.* "Masking its dangers with calm" (V.); "hiding his cruel nature" (Schmidt). "Moist" and "vast" have been suggested. V. considers *mask'd* "singularly Shakespearian in manner."

SCENE IV.—2. *Coffer.* We suspect, as D. says he does, that this should be "coffin."

3. *Character.* Handwriting. Cf. *Cymb.* p. 188.

6. *Eaning time.* Time of delivery. Cf. *M. of V.* i. 3. 88: "Who then conceiving did in eaning time," etc. The quartos have "learning time."

14. *Your date.* Your appointed term of life.

17. *That's all.* Fleay reads "and that is all."

ACT IV.

GOWER'S PROLOGUE.—8. *Music, letters.* The early eds. have "musicks letters;" corrected by Malone.

10. *Her . . . heart.* The early eds. have "hie" (or "high") . . . "art;" corrected by Steevens.

12. *Wrack.* See on ii. prol. 32 above.

14. *Seeks.* The early eds. have "Seeke" or "Seek;" corrected by Rowe.

15, 16. The early eds. have "our Cleon hath" and "a full growne wench;" corrected by Steevens. H. reads:

> "Seeks to take off by treason's knife,
> And in his kind. Cleon doth own
> One daughter, and a wench full-grown," etc.

His here is taken to refer to *envy.* "Cleon doth own" was suggested by Mr. P. A. Daniel.

17. *Rite.* The early eds. have "sight;" corrected by Coll. Percy had conjectured "rites." Malone reads "fight" (suggested by Steevens, who also proposed "night"). They think "marriage fight" may mean "Cupid's wars" or "the combats of Venus;" but, as D. says, if it meant anything it would be "matrimonial quarrels." K. (2d ed.) has "right for marriage rite;" the "right" being from the 1st quarto.

18. *Hight.* Is named. Cf. *L. L. L.* p. 131.

21. *She.* The early eds. have "they;" corrected by Malone.

Sleided=untwisted or unwrought. Cf. *L. C.* 48: "with sleided silk," etc.

23. *Needle.* Malone reads "neeld," which may be right. Cf. *M. N. D.* p. 165, note on *Needles.*

26. *Night-bird.* The early eds. have "night bed;" corrected by Malone.

27. *Records.* Sings; again used of the nightingale in *T. G. of V.* v. 4. 6. See our ed. p. 151.

29. *Vail.* Bow, do homage. See on ii. 3. 42 above.

31. *Absolute.* Faultless, perfect. Cf. *Ham.* v. 2. 111: "an absolute gentleman," etc.

32. *With the dove*, etc. The early eds. have "The Doue of Paphos might with the crow." The transposition was suggested by Mason.

For *Paphos* as sacred to Venus, cf. *Temp.* iv. 1. 93 and *V. and A.* 1193.

33. *Vie.* Compete in. Cf. iii. 1. 26 above.

40. *Stead.* See on iii. prol. 21 above.

44. *Pregnant.* Ready, apt. See *Lear*, p. 198.

45. *Prest.* Prompt, ready. Cf. *M. of V.* p. 130.

46. *I do commend to your content.* "I trust will prove to your satisfaction" (Clarke).

47. *Carry.* The early eds. have "carried;" corrected by Steevens.

51. *Does.* The reading of the 1st quarto; "doth" in the other early eds.

SCENE I.—5. *Inflaming love i' thy bosom.* The 1st quarto reads: "in flaming, thy loue bosome;" which is followed substantially by the other early eds. ("inflaming" in folios). Malone reads "inflame love in thy bosom;" Sr. "inflaming love, thy bosom;" and H. "cold, enforcing law, thy bosom." Coll. conjectures "infusing love in thy bosom." The text is due to K. and is adopted by the Camb. editors, D., Clarke, and W. It is on the whole the least unsatisfactory of the attempts to mend a hopelessly corrupt passage. H. sees an inconsistency in speaking of a *cold* conscience as *inflaming* love; but, as Clarke notes, Dionyza is urging him to let it remain cold, or "lie dead, and not let it kindle into sparks of compunction."

6. *Inflame too nicely.* Malone conjectured that these words should be omitted. Coll. and H. change *Inflame* to "Inform." *Nicely*=scrupulously, or squeamishly.

11. *Her old nurse's death.* The early eds. have "onely Mistresse death," with slight orthographical variations. The text is the conjecture of Percy. W. reads "her only nurse's death."

14. *Tellus.* Cf. *Ham.* iii. 2. 166: "Tellus' orbed ground." *Weed*=garment, dress; as in *M. N. D.* ii. 1. 256, ii. 2. 71, etc. Fleay fills out the measure by reading "rob robed [rob'd] Tellus."

17. *Carpet.* Steevens's conjecture of "chaplet" is plausible, but carpets were often used as table covers, drapery, etc. See *T. of S.* p. 154. K. remarks: "It is evident that the Poet was thinking of the *green* mound that marks the last resting-place of the humble, and not of the sculptured tomb to be adorned with wreaths. Upon the grassy grave Marina will hang a *carpet* of flowers—she will *strew* flowers, she has before said. The *carpet* of Shakespeare's time was a piece of tapestry, or embroidery, spread upon tables; and the real flowers with which Marina will cover the grave of her friend might have been, in her imagination, so intertwined as to resemble a carpet, usually bright with the flowers of the needle."

18. *Ay me.* Changed by Malone, H., and others to "Ah me," which S. never uses. See *M. N. D.* p. 128.

23–30. Here, as in many other passages of the play, the lines of the early eds. have been variously rearranged by the modern editors; but we have not thought it necessary to record the variations. We have adopted here the arrangement of the Camb. editors in the Globe ed. (in the Camb. ed. they follow the early eds.).

23. *Do not consume your blood*, etc. Alluding to the old notion that each sigh took a drop of blood from the heart. Cf. *M. N. D.* p. 163, note on 97.

25. *Favour.* Countenance, aspect; as often. See *M. N. D.* p. 130. Cf. *well favour'd* in 86 below.

27. *Ere the sea mar them.* The early eds. have "it" for *them*, which is due to K. H. reads "Give me your flowers: on the sea-margent walk," etc. Fleay would read and arrange thus:

> "Come, go you on the beach, give me your flowers.
> Ere the sea mar it, walk with Leonine."

28. *Quick.* Fresh, bracing.

29. *Sharpens.* H. reads "will sharp."

36. *Paragon to all reports.* "Whose beauty was once equal to all fame said of it" (Malone).

40. *Reserve.* Save, guard. Walker conjectures "preserve."

55. *Haling ropes.* Malone reads "with hauling of the ropes."

62. *A canvas-climber.* "One who climbs the mast to furl or unfurl the *canvas*, or sails" (Steevens).

63. *Dropping.* Coll. conjectures "dripping," to which the word is equivalent.

64. *Stem to stern.* The quartos have "sterne to sterne," and the folios "stern to stern;" corrected by Malone.

77. *La.* The first three quartos have "law," the other early eds. "now;" corrected by Malone. For the use of *la* to emphasize a statement, see *Cor.* p. 205.

97. *Valdes.* Malone suggests that the Spanish Armada furnished S. with this name. Don Pedro de Valdes was an admiral in that fleet, and was taken by Sir Francis Drake. Giving the name to a pirate would be likely to "take" with an audience of that day.

SCENE II.—This scene, which we have much abridged, could not have been written by S. See p. 28 above.

6. *Chequins.* The early eds. have "checkins," "chickins," "chickeens," or "chickens;" corrected by Malone. The *chequin* (Italian *zecchino*) was a gold coin of Venice, worth about two dollars in our money.

Were as pretty a proportion, etc. "Would be as pretty a competence as need be to live quietly with, and so give over our present occupation" (Clarke).

11. *Wages not with.* Does not equal. Cf. *A. and C.* p. 210, note on *Wag'd.*

12. *Keep our door hatched.* That is, closed against customers by means

of the half-door or *hatch;* for which see *M. W.* p. 145, note on *Pickt-hatch.*

21. *I have gone through,* etc. "I have bid a high price for her, gone far in my attempt to purchase her" (Steevens). Malone changes *through* to "thorough;" but the meaning would be the same with either word. Cf. iv. 3. 35 below.

22. *My earnest.* That is, the money given to close the bargain.

28. *I cannot be bated,* etc. Malone plausibly conjectures that it is the Pirate who says this. If it belongs to Boult, it must mean, "I cannot get them to bate," etc. D. suggests that *I* should be "It." For *doit,* cf. *M. of V.* p. 136.

40. *Fault.* Misfortune. Cf. *M. W.* p. 131. Coll. conjectures "The worse my fate."

48. *An honest woman, or not a woman.* Horn (see p. 26 above) thinks that this must be Shakespeare's; but it does not strike us as being of such exceptional character. Touches of equal "poetical profundity" are by no means rare in contemporary dramatists.

Scene III.—11. *If thou hadst drunk to him,* etc. That is, if you had poisoned yourself in pledging him.

12. *Fact.* Deed. Some make it = "crime;" but cf. *W. T.* p. 175. The word here was suggested by D. in place of the "face" of the early eds. Mason conjectures "feat."

17. *Pious.* The early quartos have "impious," the other early eds. omit the word. Mason's conjecture of *pious* is confirmed by Wilkins's novel.

18. *For an honest attribute.* For the sake of an honest reputation, or of being accounted honest.

24. *Strain.* Stock, race. See *J. C.* p. 176.

27. *Prime consent.* The early quartos have "prince consent," the other early eds. "whole consent;" corrected by D. Steevens conjectures "pre-consent."

28. *Sources.* The early eds. have "courses;" corrected by D.

30. *Can know.* Walker conjectures "can now know;" but the measure is probably to be filled out by modifying the pronunciation of *Leonine.* Proper names are often contracted for the sake of the metre (see Gr. 469), and occasionally lengthened.

31. *Distain.* Cf. *T. and C.* i. 3. 241: "distains his worth," etc. The early eds. have "disdaine" or "disdain," which Clarke retains, making it = cause to be disdained. *Distain* was the conjecture of Steevens, though Sr. was the first to adopt it. He has been followed by D., W., the Camb. ed., H., and others.

34. *Blurted at.* Treated scornfully. Malone quotes *Edw. III.:* "And all the world will blurt and scorn at us."

Malkin. "A coarse wench" (Steevens). See *Cor.* p. 223. The old spelling "mawkin" indicates the common pronunciation.

35. *Thorough.* Used by S. interchangeably with *through.* Gr. 478.

38. *It greets me.* It gratifies me. Clarke takes it to be = it comes before me, it seems to me. Malone suspects that the passage is corrupt.

46. *Thou art like the harpy*, etc. The sense is clear, though the construction is confused, as in many other passages in S. Cf. Gr. 415. Malone changes *with* to "wear." H. "fixes up" the passage thus:

> "Which, to betray, doth use an angel's face,
> Then seize with eagle's talons."

48. *Talons.* All the early eds. spell it "talents." Cf. *L. L. L.* p. 146, note on *If a talent be a claw.*

49. *You are like one*, etc. "You are so affectedly humane that you would appeal to heaven against the cruelty of winter in killing the flies" (Boswell). Clarke thinks it means: "You are like one that with over-scrupulous and superfluous explicitness assures the gods that winter kills the flies;" but this does not seem to us so natural or so forcible a retort as the other interpretation gives. Cleon has said, "You are treacherously cruel;" Dionyza replies, "You are superstitiously humane."

V. remarks: "Throughout this whole scene, slight and sketchy as it is, the reader cannot but be strongly reminded of Macbeth and his wife. Cleon's 'infirmity of purpose,' shocked at the crime, and willing to give 'the spacious world to undo the deed,' while he immediately yields to his wife's energy of guilty will, and follows out her leading, is in the same spirit with Macbeth's—

> 'I am afraid to think what I have done;
> Look on 't again I dare not,' etc.

The stern, sustained resolution of Lady Macbeth, her complaint for her husband's scruples, as—

> 'What beast was 't, then,
> That made you break this enterprise to me?'—

and her—

> 'things without remedy
> Should be without regard,'—

are, when compared with Dionyza's cool reply, 'that she 's dead,' and her—

> 'I do shame
> To think of what a noble strain you are,
> And what a coward spirit,'—

like the finished work of some great painter by the side of the first rough, spirited outline, in which he had embodied his conceptions."

SCENE IV.—2. *Cockles.* Malone sees here an allusion to the stories of witches sailing in a cockle or mussel shell.

Have an wish but for 't. Have, if we but wish for it; we have but to wish and have it.

3. *Making.* Used in the familiar nautical sense of sailing, going. Cf. v. 1. 19 below. *Take*=captivate.

Your. The old eds. have "our;" corrected by Malone.

8. *Stand i' the.* The early eds. have "stand with" or "stand in;" corrected by Steevens.

13–16. The 1st quarto, followed substantially by the other early eds., disarranges the passage thus:

> "Old *Helicanus* goes along behind,
> Is left to gouerne it, you beare in mind.
> Old *Escenes*, whom *Helicanus* late
> Aduancde in time to great and hie estate."

The arrangement in the text was proposed by Steevens. In 16 Walker conjectures "Good" for *Old*. See *Addenda*, p. 163 below.

18. *His pilot.* The early eds. have "this Pilot" or "this Pilate;" corrected by Malone. Clarke retains "this," explaining thus: "Let your imagination conceive this thought that I suggest to you; and which, like a pilot, shall conduct and accompany Pericles on his sea-voyage." The meaning of the passage as we give it is: "Suppose that your imagination is his pilot" (Malone).

19. *Grow on.* The early eds. have "grone;" corrected by Malone.

24. *Passion.* Grief, sorrow (as in the stage-direction just above). Cf. *Ham.* p. 212.

30. *His mortal vessel.* His body. Steevens quotes *A. and C.* v. 2. 51: "this mortal house I'll ruin."

31. *Wit.* Know, understand. Cf. "to wit" (*M. of V.* ii. 9. 90, etc.), which we still use as =namely.

The reading of 31–33 is that of the first three quartos. The other early eds. have:

> "Now take we our way
> To the Epitaph for Marina, writ by Dionizia."

39. *Thetis, being proud*, etc. For *Thetis* as an impersonation of the sea, cf. *T. and C.* i. 3. 39:

> "But let the ruffian Boreas once enrage
> The gentle Thetis," etc.

See our ed. p. 169.

"The poet ascribes the swelling of the sea to the pride which Thetis felt at the birth of Marina in her element; and supposes that the earth, being afraid to be overflowed, bestowed this birth-child of Thetis on the heavens; and that Thetis, in revenge, makes raging battery against the shores" (Mason).

48. *Scene.* The early eds. have "Steare," "stteare," or "stear;" corrected by Malone. Steevens reads "scenes display."

SCENE V.—7. *Shall 's.* Shall us; a colloquialism, for which see *W. T.* p. 156, or Gr. 215. Here it is the reading of the early quartos, changed to "shall we" in the other old eds.

SCENE VI.—4. *That.* So that; as in v. prol. 7 below. Gr. 283.

9. *How a*, etc. How *go* a, or how *sell* a, etc. Cf. 2 *Hen. IV.* iii. 2. 42: "How a good yoke of bullocks at Stamford fair?"

10. *To-bless.* The editors generally follow Tyrwhitt in considering this an instance of the intensive particle *to*. See on iii. 2. 17 above.

13. *Iniquity.* The reading of the early quartos; "impurity" in the other old eds. The Camb. ed. follows the quartos in making *iniquity* the object of *have.* The inversion is awkward, and we prefer Malone's pointing.

18. *For flesh and blood*, etc. The early eds. give this to Boult, but W. is clearly right in transferring it to the Bawd. The mistake probably arose, as he suggested, from using *B.* as the abbreviation of both *Bawd* and *Boult* in the MS.

54. *Persever.* The regular form of the word in S. Cf. *M. N. D.* p. 166, Gr. 492. *Clear*=pure, virtuous.

56. *Thoughten.* Thinking. For the form, cf. *foughten* in *Hen. V.* iv. 6. 18, and see Gr. 344. For the active use, see Gr. 374 (cf. 294).

59. *A piece of virtue.* Cf. *Temp.* i. 2. 56: "Thy mother was a piece of virtue;" and *A. and C.* iii. 2. 28:

> "the piece of virtue which is set
> Betwixt us as the cement of our love."

85. *Yet better.* Malone reads "better yet."

87. *Would own a name too dear.* Would think his name dishonoured.

ACT V.

Gower's Prologue.—5. *Dumbs.* Cf. *A. and C.* i. 5. 50: "Was beastly dumb'd by him."

For *needle* the early quartos have "neele," and Malone prints "neeld." See on iv. prol. 23 above.

7. *That.* So that; as in 9 just below. Cf. iv. 6. 4 above.

8. *Inkle.* The word means tape (cf. *W. T.* p. 196), but here it must be either a very narrow tape or some kind of thread used in embroidery For *twin* the early eds. have "Twine;" corrected by Malone.

13. *On the sea*, etc. The early quartos have "on the sea, wee there him left;" the other early eds. "at sea, tumbled and tost;" corrected by Malone.

14. *Whence.* The early eds. have "Where" or "And;" corrected by Steevens.

19. *His.* Changed by H. to "Her" (the conjecture of Walker); but, as Clarke suggests, the word may refer to Pericles.

21. *In your supposing*, etc. Once more imagine that you see the sorrowful Pericles. Some join *Of heavy Pericles* to what follows, reading "the bark."

23. *Where what is done*, etc. Where all that is acted—more should be shown if it were possible—shall be exhibited.

Scene I.—1. *Resolve.* Inform. See on ii. 5. 68 above. For *Helicanus* Walker conjectures "Helicane."

10. *Greet them.* The early quartos have "greet him," which the Camb. editors and Clarke retain; but the use of *some* in the singular would be anomalous.

15. *Sir.* Omitted in the early eds. and supplied by Malone.

19. *Made.* Cf. iv. 4. 3 above.

26. *Prorogue.* The reading of the early quartos; "prolong" in the other early eds.

27. *Distemperature.* Disorder. Cf. *M. N. D.* p. 144.

34. *Yet let me*, etc. The early quartos confuse the context thus:

> "*Hell.* You may, but bootlesse. Is your sight see, will not speake to any, yet let me obtaine my wish.
> *Lys.* Behold him, this was a goodly person.
> *Hell.* Till the disaster that one mortall wight droue him to this."

The arrangement was corrected in the 4th quarto; but "wight" for *night* was left to be rectified by Malone.

46. *Deafen'd.* The early eds. have "defend" or "defended;" corrected by Malone.

49. *And with her fellow maids is.* The early eds. omit *with* and *is*, both of which Malone supplied. *Upon* is changed by Steevens to "within," but the meaning may be "upon the leafy and sheltered spot," as Clarke suggests.

51. The stage-direction is not in the early eds., but was supplied by Malone.

52. *All's.* The early eds. have only "all;" corrected by Malone.

58. *Gods.* The early eds. have "God;" corrected by D. (the conjecture of Walker).

59. *Graff.* Graft; as in *R. of L.* 1062: "This bastard graff shall never come to growth." Cf. the verb in *A. Y. L.* iii. 2. 124, 2 *Hen. IV.* v. 3. 3, etc.

60. *Afflict.* The early eds. have "inflict," but it is pretty certainly one of the many misprints that disfigure them. *Afflict* was suggested by Malone, and is adopted by D., Coll., Sr., Clarke, and H.

63. The stage-direction in the early eds. is simply "*Enter Marina.*" Malone remarks: "It appears that when *Pericles* was originally performed, the theatres were furnished with no such apparatus as, by any stretch of imagination, could be supposed to present either a sea or a ship; and that the audience were contented to behold vessels sailing in and out of port in their *mind's eye* only. This license being once granted to the poet, the lord, in the instance now before us, walked off the stage, and returned again in a few minutes, leading in Marina without any sensible impropriety; and the present drama exhibited before such indulgent spectators was not more incommodious in the representation than any other would have been."

65. *Presence.* The early eds. have "present;" corrected by Malone.

67. *Came of*, etc. Not more elliptical than many passages in the play; but Steevens reads "she came Of gentle kind," etc.

69. *Fair one, all.* The early eds. have "Faire on all" or "Faire and all;" corrected by Malone. *Bounty* is Steevens's conjecture for the "beautie" or "beauty" of the early eds.

71. *Prosperous and artificial feat.* "Felicitous accomplishment, gracefully and skilfully performed deed" (Clarke). For *feat* the early eds. have "fate;" corrected by Steevens (the conjecture of Percy), who also reads "prosperous-artificial." Cf. *M. for M.* i. 2. 189:

> "beside, she hath prosperous art
> When she will play with reason and discourse,
> And well she can persuade."

75. *Recovery.* Walker conjectures "recure," which H. adopts.

79. *Marina sings.* The following is Marina's song, according to Twine (quoted by Steevens):

"Amongst the harlots foul I walk,
  Yet harlot none am I;
The rose among the thorns it grows,
  And is not hurt thereby.

The thief that stole me, sure I think,
  Is slain before this time;
A bawd me bought, yet am I not
  Defil'd by fleshly crime.

Were nothing pleasanter to me
  Than parents mine to know;
I am the issue of a king,
  My blood from kings doth flow.

I hope that God will mend my state,
  And send a better day:
Leave off your tears, pluck up your heart,
  And banish care away.

Show gladness in your countenance,
  Cast up your cheerful eyes:
That God remains that once of nought
  Created earth and skies.
He will not let, in care and thought,
You still to live, and all for nought."

Wilkins, in his novel, quotes this with the following variations:

"The rose among the thorns doth grow."

"Nothing were pleasanter to me."

"In time the heavens may mend my state,
  And send a better day;
For sorrow adds unto our griefs,
  But helps not any way."

The closing couplet is omitted by Wilkins.

The song is a translation of the following hexameters in the *Gesta Romanorum* (quoted, with some corrections, by Malone):

"Per scorta heu! gradior, sed scorti conscia non sum:
Sic spinis rosa quae nescit violarier ullis.
Corruit en raptor gladii ferientis ab ictu;
Tradita lenoni non sum violata pudore.
Vulnera cessassent animi, lacrimaeque deessent,
Nulla ergo melior, si noscam certa parentes.
Unica regalis generis sum stirpe creata;
Ipsa jubente Deo. laetari credo aliquando.
Terge modo lacrimas, curam dissolve molestam;
Redde polo faciem, mentemque ad sidera tolle:
Nam Deus est hominum plasmator, rector, et auctor,
Nec sinit has lacrimas casso finire labore."

93. *Awkward.* Adverse. Cf. 2 *Hen. VI.* p. 165.

100. *You would not do me violence.* Referring to the manner in which he at first repulsed her, and to which he alludes in 126 below. Some believe that a portion of the text has been lost here. According to Twine, the king "rose up sodainly and *stroke* the maiden," etc.

103. *Shores.* The early eds. have "shews" or "shewes;" corrected by Malone (the conjecture of the Earl of Charlemont).

106. *I am great with woe*, etc. Malone compares *Rich. II.* ii. 2. 62 fol.

112. *Who starves*, etc. Cf. *A. and C.* ii. 2. 241:

> "other women cloy
> The appetites they feed, but she makes hungry
> Where most she satisfies."

117. *Owe.* Own, possess; as very often. The meaning is: "These endowments, however valuable in themselves, are heightened by being in your possession; they acquire additional grace from their owner" (Steevens).

121. *Palace.* The early eds. have "Pallas;" corrected by Malone.

126. *Say.* The early eds. have "stay;" corrected by Malone.

132. *Open'd.* Fleay adds "justly" (from 88 above).

135. *Thousandth.* Malone's correction of the "thousand" of the early eds.

138. *Like Patience*, etc. Cf. *T. N.* ii. 4. 117:

> "She sat like Patience on a monument,
> Smiling at grief."

Smiling extremity out of act. "By her beauty and patient meekness disarming calamity" (Malone). For *extremity*=the utmost of suffering, cf. *Lear*, v. 3. 207: "And top extremity."

140. *How lost thou them? Thy name*, etc. The early eds. have "How lost thou thy name," etc.; corrected by Malone.

155. *No motion?* "That is, no puppet dressed up to deceive me?" (Steevens). Cf. *T. G. of V.* ii. 1. 100: "O excellent motion! O exceeding puppet!" See our ed. p. 130. *No*, omitted in the early eds., was supplied by Steevens. K. adopts the conjecture of Mason:

> "and are no fairy-motion?
> Well, speak on," etc.

D. takes "Motion!" to be the exclamation of Pericles after feeling of Marina's pulse. W. conjectures that the "Motion" of the early eds. is a stage-direction that has got into the text.

157. *For.* Because. Cf. ii. 1. 70 above.

161. *Deliver'd.* Related. Cf. 169 just below.

167. *You'll scarce believe me.* The early eds. have "You scorn, believe me;" which the Camb. editors and W. retain, with a colon after "scorn." St. reads "You scorn to believe me." The text is Malone's, and is adopted by D. and H.

174. *Who having drawn to do't.* Clarke conjectures "he being drawn" (cf. *Temp.* ii. 1. 308, etc.); but "who being drawn" would be better, we think, if any change is made for the sake of the metre. Steevens omitted *to do't*, leaving the rest of the line as it is.

188. *Would never.* The early eds. have "never would;" corrected by Steevens.

207, 208. *Thou hast been*, etc. The 1st quarto, followed substantially by the other early eds., reads:

> "Thou hast beene God-like perfit, the heir of kingdomes,
> And an other like to *Pericles* thy father."

The passage is probably mutilated, and many attempts have been made to restore it. A page and a half of the Camb. ed. is devoted to recording them. The most plausible is Mason's:

> "thou 'rt heir of kingdoms,
> And another life to Pericles thy father;"

which we adopt with the modification in the arrangement of the lines made by D., H., and others. Cf. what Pericles has said in 196 just above. Malone (ed. 1790) reads:

> "(as in the rest you said
> Thou hast been godlike-perfect) the heir of kingdoms,
> And a mother like to Pericles thy father;"

making *heir* refer to *queen*. Sr. (2d ed) has

> "the heir of kingdoms,
> And another life to Pericles thy father."

Coll. follows this, except that he has "thou heir;" and St. also, except that he prints "another-life."

226. *Doubt.* The early eds. have "doat" or "dote;" corrected by Malone.

230. *The music of the spheres.* Cf. *T. N.* iii. 1. 121: "Than music from the spheres;" and see *A. Y. L.* p. 162, note on *The spheres.*

232. *Music, my lord?* etc. The early quartos have "*Lys.* Musicke my Lord? I heare." The later ones point it thus: "Musicke my Lord, I heare." (except that the 6th has an interrogation mark instead of the period); and the folios thus: "Musick, my Lord, I hear." Malone and Clarke read "Music? My lord, I hear—" D. suggested that *Music* should be printed as a stage-direction, and in this he has been followed by St., W., and Delius. The arrangement of the passage in the text was suggested by the Camb. editors, who remark: "No music is mentioned in Wilkins's novel, and any music of earth would be likely to jar with that 'music of the spheres' which was already lulling Pericles to sleep." H. also adopts this reading.

234. *Nips.* A suspicious word, for which Coll. proposes "raps" (cf. *Cymb.* p. 176).

236. *A pillow*, etc. Sr. gives this speech to Marina (Malone's conjecture); but, as Clarke remarks, "the tone of direction and command is more suitable to the governor of Mytilene than to the young girl Marina, princess though she be; and the unassured conviction implied in '*If* this but answer to my just belief,' rather befits the admirer of Marina than Marina herself, who is thoroughly aware that she is none other than Pericles' own daughter."

240. *Diana appears*, etc. Most editors begin a new scene here; but the Camb. ed., W., and H. follow D. in continuing the scene.

Fleay says that he regards this little episode of Diana as no more Shakespeare's work than the vision in *Cymbeline* (see our ed. p. 215, note on 30); and we are inclined to agree with him.

246. *Life.* The early eds. have "like;" corrected by Malone (the conjecture of the Earl of Charlemont).

247. *Or perform.* Malone omits *Or.*

248. *Do it, and happy.* That is, thou *livest* happy. The early eds. have "doo't" or "do't," and Malone reads "Do't, and be happy."

250. *Argentine.* "Silver-shining" (*R. of L.* 786); used by S. only here. Malone quotes Lord Charlemont's remark that "in the chemical phrase, a language well understood when this play was written, Luna or *Diana* means *silver*, as Sol does gold;" but silver had been associated with Diana and the moon long before the days of the alchemists.

255. *Blown.* "Swollen" (Steevens).

261. *Suit.* The early eds. have "sleight;" corrected by Malone.

SCENE II.—Those who begin a new scene at the appearance of Diana (line 240 of preceding scene) continue it through this speech of Gower's. D. includes the speech in scene 1.

2. *Dumb.* The early eds. have "dum," except the 4th folio, which gives "dun." Rowe reads "done."

3. *My last boon.* Malone reads "as my last boon" (the conjecture of Steevens). D. suggests "deign to give," and St. "freely give." H. reads "pray you, give."

12. *He had done.* "That is, *Pericles* had done" (Malone).

14. *Confound.* Consume; as in 1 *Hen. IV.* i. 3. 100: "He did confound the best part of an hour," etc.

20. *Fancies'.* The early eds. have "fancies;" and Rowe reads "fancy's." For "doom" (the early reading) Steevens, followed by some recent editors, has "boon;" but the rhyme of *soon* and *doom* is no worse than *run* and *dumb* in 1 and 2 above and many others in these Gower prologues. In iii. prol. 31, 32, we have *moons* and *dooms.* *Thankful doom*=thankworthy judgment or decree.

SCENE III.—6. *Who.* All the early eds. except the 4th folio have "whom."

8. *Who.* Malone reads "whom;" as in 57 below. See on i. 4. 34 above.

13. *Favour.* Face, looks; as in iv. 1. 25 above.

15. *Nun.* The early quartos have "mum," the other old eds. "woman." *Nun* is the reading of Coll. According to the Camb. ed. it is also given by a MS. corrector in Capell's copy of the 1st quarto. It is confirmed by Wilkins's novel.

22. *In blustering morn.* The reading of the early eds., for which Malone suggests "one."

24. *There.* The reading of the early quartos; "these" in the other old eds.

36. *Drown'd.* That is, sunk and lost in the water. Cf. *Temp.* v. 1. 57: "I 'll drown my book," etc.

38. *Parted.* Parted from, left; as in *Rich. II.* iii. 1. 3: "your souls must part your bodies." Gr. 198.

41. *You shall do well,* etc. Malone compares *Oth.* ii. 1. 191:

> "If it were now to die,
> 'T were now to be most happy;"

and *W. T.* iv. 4. 472:

> "If I might die within this hour, I have liv'd
> To die when I desire."

43. *Be buried*, etc. Cf. *W. T.* iv. 4. 132:

> "not to be buried,
> But quick and in my arms."

48. *For.* Because. Cf. v. 1. 157 above.

57. *Who.* Malone reads "whom." Cf. 8 above.

59. *This man.* D. and H. adopt Walker's plausible conjecture, "this is the man."

61. *Resolve.* Satisfy, inform; as in v. 1. 13 above.

63. *Deliver.* State, tell. See on v. 1. 161 above.

74. *Makes.* The reading of the early quartos; "that makes" in the other old eds. and in some modern ones. Gr. 244. The speech is evidently corrupt.

79. *Make a star of him.* Honour him with a place among the stars. Steevens cites *R. and J.* iii. 2. 22:

> "when he shall die,
> Take him and cut him out in little stars;"

and *Cymb.* v. 5. 352:

> "for they are worthy
> To inlay heaven with stars."

See also 1 *Hen. VI.* i. 1. 55:

> "A far more glorious star thy soul will make
> Than Julius Cæsar or bright—"

89. *Preserv'd.* The early eds. have "preferd" or "preferred;" corrected by Malone.

96. *The honour'd.* The quarto reading; "and" for *the* in the folios.

97. *City.* Of course =citizens, as Malone informs us.

98. *That.* So that. Cf. iv. 6. 4 above.

100. *Punish them.* The early eds. omit *them*, which Malone supplied. H. reads "punish crime."

ADDENDA.

THE "TIME-ANALYSIS" OF THE PLAY.—This is summed up by Mr. P. A. Daniel (*Trans. of New Shaks. Soc.* for 1877–79, p. 255), thus:

"The story of *Pericles* comprises a period of from fifteen to sixteen years, of which fourteen days are represented on the stage, the chief intervals being accounted for in the choruses."

1st Chorus, introducing—

Day 1. Act I. sc. i.

Interval. Pericles returns to Tyre.

" 2. Act I. sc. ii., iii.

Interval. Pericles sails to Tarsus.

Day 3. Act I. sc. iv.

2d Chorus. An *interval:* Sojourn of Pericles at Tarsus, departure therefrom, and arrival at Pentapolis.

Day 4. Act II. sc. i.
" 5. Act II. sc. ii.–iv.
" 6. Act II. sc. v.

3d Chorus. An *interval* of eight or nine months: marriage of Pericles, his wedded life, and departure from Pentapolis.

Day 7. Act III. sc. i.
" 8. Act III. sc. ii.
Interval: A few days.
" 9. Act III. sc. iii., iv.

4th Chorus. An *interval* of fourteen years: education of Marina in Tarsus.

Day 10. Act IV. sc. i.
Interval. Marina's voyage from Tarsus to Mytilene.
" 11. Act IV. sc. ii., iii.

5th Chorus. Act IV. sc. iv. An *interval* of a few days: Pericles arrives in Tarsus, and departs therefrom on learning his daughter's supposed death.

Day 12. Act IV. sc. v., vi. [should be V. i., ii.]

6th Chorus. An *interval* of three months between the departure of Pericles from Tarsus and his arrival at Mytilene.

Day 13. Act V. sc. i.

7th Chorus. Act. V. sc. ii. An *interval.* Sojourn in Mytilene and voyage to Ephesus.

Day 14. Act V. sc. iii.

8th Chorus. Epilogue.

List of the Characters in the Play, with the Scenes in which they Appear.—The numbers in parentheses indicate the lines the characters have in each scene.

Antiochus: i. 1(67). Whole no. 67.
Pericles: i. 1(98), 2(94), 4(17); ii. 1(79), 3(25), 5(33); iii. 1(59), 3(28); v. 1(115), 3(55). Whole no. 603.
Helicanus: i. 2(31), 3(19); ii. 4(32); v. 1(39), 3(1). Whole no. 122.
Escanes: ii. 4(2). Whole no. 2.
Simonides: ii. 2(28), 3(67), 5(58). Whole no. 153.
Cleon: i. 4(74); iii. 3(14); iv. 3(22). Whole no. 110.
Lysimachus: iv. 6(52); v. 1(55). Whole no. 107.
Cerimon: iii. 2(84), 4(8); v. 3(17). Whole no. 109.
Thaliard: i. 1(6), 3(22) Whole no. 28.
Philemon: iii 2(3). Whole no. 3.
Leonine: iv. 1(23). Whole no. 23.
Marshal: ii. 3(1). Whole no. 1.

Pandar: iv. 2(28), 6(4). Whole no. 32.
Boult: iv. 2(44), 6(55). Whole no. 99.
Messenger: i. 1(1). Whole no. 1.
1st Lord: i. 2(1), 4(7); ii. 2(6), 4(16); v. 1(3). Whole no. 33.
2d Lord: i. 2(2); ii. 2(2), 4(7). Whole no. 11.
3d Lord: ii. 2(2), 4(1). Whole no. 3.
1st Fisherman: ii. 1(43). Whole no. 43.
2d Fisherman: ii. 1(31). Whole no. 31.
3d Fisherman: ii. 1(20). Whole no. 20.
1st Knight: ii. 3(6), 5(1). Whole no. 7.
2d Knight: ii. 5(1). Whole no. 1.
3d Knight: ii. 5(1). Whole no. 1.
1st Sailor: iii. 1(10). Whole no. 10.
2d Sailor: iii. 1(6). Whole no. 6.
1st Gentleman: iii. 2(18); iv. 5(6); v. 1(1). Whole no. 25.
2d Gentleman: iii. 2(14); iv. 5(4). Whole no. 18.
1st Pirate: iv. 1(1), 2(1). Whole no. 2.
2d Pirate: iv. 1(1). Whole no. 1.
3d Pirate: iv. 1(2). Whole no. 2.
Servant: iii. 2(6). Whole no. 6.
Tyrian Sailor: v. 1(9). Whole no. 9.
Daughter (of Antiochus): i. 1(2). Whole no. 2.
Dionyza: i. 4(9); iii. 3(6); iv. 1(38), 3(36). Whole no. 89.
Thaisa: ii. 2(22), 3(22), 5(4); iii. 2(2), 4(10); v. 3(22). Whole no. 82.
Marina: iv. 1(46), 2(16), 6(61); v. 1(65), 3(2). Whole no. 190.
Lychorida: iii. 1(11). Whole no. 11.
Bawd: iv. 2(74), 6(43). Whole no. 117.
"*Diana*": v. 1(10). Whole no. 10.
"*Gower*" (*as* "*Chorus*"): i. (42); ii. (40); iii. (60); iv. (52), 4(51); v. (24), 2(20), 3(18). Whole no. 307.
"*All*": i. 4(2); ii. 2(1), 4(1). Whole no. 4.

In the above enumeration, parts of lines are counted as whole lines, making the total in the play greater than it is. The actual number of lines in each scene (Globe edition numbering) is as follows: i. chor. (42), 1(171), 2(124), 3(40), 4(108); ii. chor. (40), 1(173), 2(60), 3(116), 4(58), 5(93); iii. chor. (60), 1(182), 2(111), 3(41), 4(18); iv. chor. (52), 1(103), 2(163), 3(51), 4(51), 5(10), 6(212); v. chor. (24), 1(265), 2(20), 3(103). Whole number of lines in the play, 2391 (in Shakespeare's part, 756).

Note on iv. 4. 13-16 (p. 153).—Mr. P. A. Daniel would retain the text of the 1st quarto, pointing it thus:

"Old Helicanus goes along. Behind
Is left to govern it, you bear in mind,
Old Escanes, whom Helicanus late
Advanc'd in time to great and high estate."

He adds that "one minute's study of the original will convince the reader that Steevens's corruption and topsy-turvy arrangement must forthwith be expunged." Possibly he is right. His pointing makes sense of the passage, and the arrangement is not clumsier than in some other parts of these choruses.

GOWER.

INDEX OF WORDS AND PHRASES EXPLAINED.